Moderation, Comportment, and Knowledge On the Path to God

Lectures of Shaykh Aḥmad al-Tijānī ʿAlī Cissé

FAYDA BOOKS

First published in 2022 by
Fayda Books llc.
1677 Dorsey Ave
East Point, GA 30344

http://www.faydabooks.com
orders@faydabooks.com

ISBN: 978-1-7339631-7-6

Printed and bound in the United States

Moderation, Comportment, and Knowledge On the Path to God

Lectures of Shaykh Aḥmad al-Tijānī ʿAlī Cissé

translated, edited, and introduced by
Zachary Wright

Atlanta, USA, and Accra, Ghana
Fayda Books
2022

Table of Contents

7. **Acknowledgments**

9. **Introduction**

25. **Peace, Tolerance, and Moderation in Islam**

51. **Rights of Women in Islam**

71. **Fraternity in God**

91. **Love for the Prophet Muḥammad**

115. **Exemplary Etiquette on the Path**

129. **Sainthood in Islam**

145. **Knowledge of God**

Acknowledgements

All praise is due to God. The translator and publisher of this volume would like to thank the Imam Shaykh al-Tijānī Cissé for his permission and patience with us in collecting, excerpting, translating, and editing his extraordinary corpus of Arabic speeches. We also acknowledge the many selfless individuals who exerted great effort in hosting the conferences and events at which these speeches were delivered. Particularly deserving of mention include Sharīf ʿUmar b. ʿAbd al-ʿAzīz who led the invitation of the Imam's colloquiums in the Ivory Coast, Dr. Bahaou Dine Som who hosted the Imam's talk in Germany, Ustādh Khalīl Niasse who organized the multiple addresses in the United Kingdom, and al-Ḥājj Elijah Mukarram and the Islamic World International Conference who facilitated the Imam's many lectures in the United States. We also thank those who contributed preliminary translations of sections of these speeches or who offered substantive advice on translation, including ʿĀdil Qamar, Ibrāhīm Nasīm, and Muḥammad ʿAbdallāh.

Zachary Wright & Ibrahim Dimson

Introduction

Biographical Portrait of Shaykh al-Tijani Cisse

By Zachary Wright

Shaykh Aḥmad al-Tijānī b. ʿAlī Cissé, or Cheikh Tidiane Cissé in the French spelling, holds the Imamate of the Grand Mosque in Medina-Baye Kaolack, Senegal. As Imam of the spiritual heart for the followers of Shaykh Ibrāhīm Niasse,[1] he is the teacher and guide of millions of Muslims around the world, particularly of the Tijāniyya Sufi order established by Shaykh Aḥmad al-Tijānī (d. 1815, Fez).[2] He succeeded to the position after a lifetime of personal instruction and companionship with some of the twentieth century's most eminent Tijānī scholars: Shaykh Ibrāhīm Niasse (d. 1975), Shaykh Sayyidī ʿAlī Cissé (d. 1982), and Shaykh Ḥasan b. ʿAlī Cissé (d. 2008). Upon succeeding to the Imamate in 2008, Shaykh al-Tijānī Cissé also assumed leadership of the humanitarian NGO founded by Shaykh Ḥasan Cissé, the African American Islamic Institute. He has more recently founded a parallel NGO to help expand the mission to promote Islamic learning, called the International Fayda Foundation. The Shaykh has attained wide renown as an Islamic scholar, a Sufi guide, and a committed humanitarian activist.

Shaykh al-Tijānī Cissé (b. 1955) is the second son of Shaykh Ibrāhīm Niasse's first daughter, Fāṭima Zahrāʾ Niasse, and his most beloved student and successor (*khalīfa*), Sayyidī ʿAlī Cissé. The Niasse family, claiming mixed Fulani and Arab descent from ʿUqba b. Nāfiʿ (d. 683),[3] came from the central Senegalese kingdom of Jolof to the more southern Saloum region of Senegal in the mid-nineteenth century to participate in the Jihad of Muḥammad Bā Diakou (d. 1867), along with the forefathers of other notable Senegalese scholars such as Shaykh Aḥmad

---

1 "Shaykh al-Islam" Ibrāhīm b. ʿAbdallāh Niasse (1900-1975, Senegal) founded a revivalist network of Islamic knowledge transmission throughout Africa and beyond, privileging the direct experiential knowledge (*maʿrifa*) of God and the importance of living scholarly exemplars. He attracted millions of adherents and new converts to Islam, attracting the attention of Middle East leaders like Gamal Abdel Nasser and King Faisal, as well as Pan-Africanist activists like Kwame Nkumah. For more, see Rüdiger Seesemann, *The Divine Flood: Ibrāhīm Niasse and the Roots of a Twentieth-Century Sufi Revival* (Oxford UP, 2011); Zachary Wright, *Living Knowledge in West African Islam: the Sufi Community of Ibrāhīm Niasse* (Brill, 2015).

2 Shaykh Aḥmad b. Maḥammad al-Tijānī (1737-1815) founded the Tijāniyya Sufi order in late eighteenth-century North Africa, according to Tijānī traditions at the command of the Prophet Muḥammad in a waking vision. Al-Tijānī was born in Ain Madi, Algeria, and passed away in Fez, Morocco, where his tomb remains a place of visitation for his followers found today all over the world, but predominately in North and West Africa. For more, see Jamil Abun-Nasr, *The Tijaniyya: A Sufi Order in the Modern World* (Oxford University Press, 1965); Zachary Wright, *Realizing Islam: the Tijāniyya in North Africa and the Eighteenth-Century Muslim World* (University of North Carolina Press, 2020).

3 Seesemann, *Divine Flood*, 156; Wright, *Living Knowledge in West African Islam*, 80.

Bamba (d. 1927). In Saloum, the Niasse were first hosted by a local scholarly family of renown, the Cissé, one of the earliest West African clerical lineages claiming descent from the Soninke kings of ancient Ghana.[4] Shaykh Ibrāhīm's father, al-Ḥājj 'Abdallāh Niasse (d. 1922), became the first scholar in the region to hold an unlimited authorization (*ijāza muṭlaqa*) in the Tijāniyya Sufi order. Sayyidī 'Alī's father, known as *al-tafsīr* Ḥasan (Ḥasan, the expert Qur'ān exegete), became al-Ḥājj 'Abdallāh's favored disciple. These two renowned scholarly lineages of the Saloum thereafter became inextricably linked, later producing some of West Africa's most notable contemporary Muslim scholars in the persons of Shaykh Ḥasan Cissé, Shaykh al-Tijānī Cissé, and Shaykh Muḥammad al-Māḥī Cissé (b. 1965).

Following the example of his ancestors, Shaykh al-Tijānī Cissé memorized the Qur'ān at an early age in Medina-Baye, Kaolack. Thereafter, he served for some time as a Qur'ān teacher in Medina-Baye while continuing his Islamic studies. In his late teens, he devoted himself full-time to personalized instruction (*majālis al-'ilm*), first under his father, Sayyidī 'Alī (1971-1972); and then under his grandfather, Shaykh Ibrāhīm (1973). He then left for Cairo, where he spent ten years studying at the prestigious Azhar University, graduating with degrees in Arabic language and literature (1974 and 1977, ranked first and fourth in his classes respectively), and in Religious Foundations (*uṣūl al-dīn*), with a specialization in Prophetic narrations (*ḥadīth*) in 1981.

Despite being only twenty years old at the time of the passing of Shaykh Ibrāhīm Niasse, Shaykh al-Tijānī Cissé was fortunate to benefit from his grandfather's instruction; just as Shaykh Ibrāhīm's young age of twenty when his own father and shaykh al-Ḥājj 'Abdallāh Niasse passed did not prevent him from a full inheritance from his father. Shaykh al-Tijānī Cissé was the last student to be personally instructed by Shaykh Ibrāhīm in the curriculum of the Islamic sciences, studying with him works of classical Arabic literature such as *Maqāmāt*

4 Wright, *Living Knowledge in West African Islam*, 105.

al-Ḥarīrī[5] and Arab poetry of the pre-Islamic era.[6] Shaykh Ibrāhīm was proud of his grandson's Qur'ān learning, charging him at a young age to review, along with Sayyidī ʿAlī and Shaykh Ibrāhīm's first son ʿAbdallāh, the memorization of eminent students in Medina-Baye.[7] Shortly thereafter, Shaykh Ibrāhīm asked his grandson to lead the supererogatory Ramadan prayers (*tarāwīḥ*) in the grand mosque of Medina-Baye, but Shaykh al-Tijānī Cissé asked permission to further pursue his learning in Cairo instead, a request his grandfather was happy to facilitate.[8]

Shaykh al-Tijānī Cissé wrote his grandfather a number of letters, at least one of which remained in Shaykh Ibrāhīm personal archive of noteworthy papers later found after his passing. Just having completed his spiritual training (*tarbiya*), the young Shaykh al-Tijānī wrote to express his gratitude at attaining the full cognizance (*maʿrifa*) of God:

> To the holy presence (*ḥaḍra*) of the noble master and respected father… As I write this letter today, my soul surges in tumultuous grief, being crushed and collapsing in on itself. My beloved master, I swear by God that I have wished to write this letter many times. But whenever I tried to write expressing to you the great thankfulness of my heart, or the deep emotions overwhelming my soul, or the longing to extol you that preoccupied my thoughts—all on account of this treasured gift that I have received from your honored presence—I found myself incapable of fulfilling the right of gratitude due to you. I perceive my pen too stunted to describe your bounty, or to express the honor due to you.[9]

---

5 The "Assemblies of al-Ḥarīrī" is the best-known work of classical Arabic literature, written by al-Qāsim al-Ḥarīrī (d. 1122, Basra).

6 These are sometimes known as *al-Muʿallaqāt* (the poems honored by being hung on the Kaʿba before the advent of Islam), and included poets such as ʿImrū al-Qays, Ṭufayl, and Labīd.

7 Evidence for this includes a letter from Shaykh Ibrāhīm naming Shaykh al-Tijānī Cissé, at the age of 15, after Sayyid ʿAlī and ʿAbdallāh for the review of ʿUmar Sharīf, the descendant of Shaykh Aḥmad al-Tijānī (d. 1815) and grandson of Shaykh Ibrāhīm, who had finished memorizing the Qur'ān in Medina-Baye May of 1970.

8 Al-Tijānī ʿAlī Cissé, interview with Zachary Wright, Medina Kaolack, Senegal, September 2008.

9 Al-Tijānī ʿAlī Cissé, letter to Ibrāhīm Niasse from Medina-Baye, Senegal, date unknown, but likely between 1973 and 1975. As cited in Wright, *Living Knowledge in West African Islam*, 184-185.

On at least one occasion, Shaykh Ibrāhīm took time out of his busy schedule to write his grandson while the young scholar was studying in Cairo:

> To the spiritual presence (*ḥaḍra*) of the cherished grandson, the master, Shaykh Aḥmad al-Tijānī ʿAlī Cissé, the honored: peace be to you and the mercy and blessing of God. I thank you heartily for your elegant greetings to me on the occasion of the most blessed month of Ramadan. Congratulations to you on the success in your exams, and on the happy celebration of the Eid. I ask God to take you by the hand, and to open to you the doors of knowledge, and to let your heart roam freely in the pastures of goodness and righteousness for ever more. I ask that God accept all of your pious prayers.[10]

Shaykh Ibrāhīm's will mentioned that the Imamate of his community should pass first to his closest disciple and inheritor Sayyidī ʿAlī Cissé, then to his grandson Ḥasan, and then to "whomever God wills."[11] But Shaykh Ibrāhīm had already alerted al-Tijānī Cissé that he would one day be the Imam. Once, one of Shaykh Ibrāhīm's children sent her young nephew al-Tijānī to her father asking for money, no doubt aware the Shaykh's fondness for his grandson. Shaykh Ibrāhīm told al-Tijānī Cissé, "One day you will be the Imam, so do not let others send you on their errands."[12] Upon his investiture as Imam following the passing of his beloved brother Shaykh Ḥasan Cissé, the eminent children of Shaykh Ibrāhīm publicly concurred that Shaykh al-Tijānī Cissé was the one "whom God wills" mentioned in the will of Shaykh Ibrāhīm.[13]

The Imam's close proximity to Shaykh Ibrāhīm was also confirmed by a number of visionary experiences. According to his own narration, once after his father had given him a powerful prayer (*duʿāʾ*) for illumination, he dreamed that he flew through the air to an inaccessible room

---

10 Shaykh Ibrāhīm Niasse, letter to Shaykh al-Tijānī Cissé in Cairo from Medina-Baye Senegal, 13 Shawwāl 1394 (30 October 1974).

11 For discussion of this will, see Wright, *Living Knowledge*, 128-129; and Hill, "Divine Knowledge," 318-330.

12 Shaykh al-Tijānī Cissé, interview with Zachary Wright, Medina Kaolack, Senegal, June 2016.

13 Witness of Zachary Wright, who was present at the ceremony of investiture in the house of Shaykh Ḥasan Cissé, August, 2008.

where Shaykh Ibrāhīm was sitting in remembrance. Not finding another way to enter, he found that God removed for him the entire ceiling of the room, and he came to sit in front of his grandfather. Startled, his grandfather told him, "Now you pray for me." In another dream after becoming Imam, he dreamed that Shaykh Ibrāhīm came to Medina-Baye and asked him permission to pray in the mosque. Upon completing the prayer, Shaykh Ibrāhīm told him, "Now I will go and leave the mosque to you." In another vision, the Imam saw himself prostrating in prayer (*sajda*) between the Prophet Muḥammad and Shaykh Ibrāhīm.[14]

Shaykh al-Tijānī Cissé had a remarkably close relationship with his father, Sayyidī ʿAlī. On the day of his son's birth, Sayyid ʿAlī wrote:

> Praise to God, who by His blessing allows good deeds to be completed. Blessing and peace on the confluence of perfection, our master Muḥammad, the locus of effusions (*fuyūḍāt*). May God be pleased with the seal of saints, our master Aḥmad al-Tijānī. Praise to God, I have had my bounty renewed with a male child by my wife, the blessed lady, Fāṭima al-Zahrāʾ daughter of our shaykh al-Ḥājj Ibrāhīm. I have named him with the name of our shaykh, the owner of the flood (*Abū l-fayḍ*), the hidden pole, our master, Shaykh Aḥmad al-Tijānī, may God be pleased with him. (This has been on) Thursday, the fifth of Ṣafar, in the year 1375, in Medina-Kaolack. And I hope God will give my son the blessing of him whom he was named after, and him who named him, and I hope that he becomes one of the people of perfection (*ahl al-kamāl*).[15]

Following the passing of Shaykh Ibrāhīm, Shaykh al-Tijānī Cissé took time away from his studies in Cairo to spend with his father, Sayyidī ʿAlī Cissé, in Medina-Baye, at one time spending six months to serve him full time in his later years. At that time, one prominent guest remarked to his father that he had not been aware that Shaykh al-Tijānī was Sayyidī ʿAlī's son because he attended to his father with the devotion and humility of

14 Dreams related by Shaykh al-Tijānī Cissé, interview with Zachary Wright, Medina Kaolack, Senegal, July, 2016; December, 2021.

15 Saydi Ali Cissé, handwritten note, dated 22 September 1955.

a disciple and servant rather than the entitlement of a child.[16] Shaykh al-Tijānī wrote his father's prayers, letters, and other discourses during this period; in part due to his beautiful Arabic penmanship. Not long before his own passing, Sayyidī ʿAlī invested his beloved son with a comprehensive authorization (*al-ijāza al-muṭlaqa*) transmitting all of his own learning:

> Praise to God the One, and peace on the last Prophet. I grant authorization to the righteous son, the prudent, well-mannered, and most esteemed scholar (*al-ʿallāma al-ḥasīb*), the master, the Shaykh Aḥmad al-Tijānī Cissé, my son and the delight of my heart. I grant him authorization just as his grandfather, the Shaykh of Islam and the happiness of humanity, Shaykh al-Ḥājj Ibrāhīm b. al-Shaykh al-Ḥājj ʿAbdallāh, authorized me, in the collection of all authorizations (*jamīʿ al-ijāzāt*). This is a complete authorization, unlimited, and a lasting inheritance until the Day of Judgment. I ask God, the Generous Lord, that He benefit him by this, and that He benefit anyone who takes knowledge from him, even if one letter. The last of our supplications is to praise God the Lord of all the worlds. Peace. This authorization was written by the father, servant of the Ibrāhīmī presence, ʿAlī Cissé b. Ḥasan, on Friday the twenty-second of Ramadan in the year 1401 (24 July 1981) in Medina Kaolack, may God protect it and cause it to endure.[17]

Shaykh al-Tijānī Cissé had a similarly close relationship to his beloved mother Sayyida Fāṭima Zahrāʾ Niasse, whom he regularly visited before her passing in 2020. She once informed him that he was precious to her as Ḥusayn was to Fāṭima, the daughter of the Prophet Muḥammad. She then related that an elder shaykh from Nigeria known for his spiritual unveiling (*kashf*) had come to visit her in Medina-Baye. He informed her by way of divine inspiration that Sayyidī ʿAlī and Fāṭima in relationship

16 Shaykh al-Tijānī Cissé, interview with Zachary Wright, Medina Kaolack, Senegal, June 2016.

17 For more discussion on the content of the authorizations acquired by Shaykh Ibrāhīm and passed to Sayyid ʿAlī, see Seesemann, *Divine Flood*, 38-41; Wright, *Living Knowledge*, 194-196.

to Shaykh Ibrāhīm were like ʿAlī b. Abī Ṭālib and Fāṭima b. Muḥammad in relationship to the Prophet Muḥammad; and that her first two sons stood in the rank of the Prophet's grandsons Ḥasan and Ḥusayn: "As for your son Shaykh al-Tijānī, he is al-Ḥusayn."[18]

Shaykh al-Tijānī continued to serve the memory of Shaykh Ibrāhīm and Sayyidī ʿAlī through his close relationship with his older brother and designated Imam, Shaykh Ḥasan Cissé. He assisted his brother's mission in service to knowledge and humanity through accompanying him in his travels, counseling him in the affairs of the community, praying for him, and editing and publishing the Arabic writings of Shaykh Ibrāhīm. It is related that he would carry his brother's luggage when traveling as would a humble disciple. For his part, Shaykh Ḥasan did not show anyone, whether king, president, or eminent shaykh, more honor in his life than he did to Shaykh al-Tijānī. He used to simply call him, "Shaykh," and anytime his younger brother would come to visit him, he would get up and either dismiss everyone else from the room or go into another room to speak with his brother in private. This was an honor he did not accord for anyone else. Shaykh Ḥasan would become angry if anyone, even from his own children, were to imply the slightest disrespect to Shaykh al-Tijānī. Before his passing, Shaykh Ḥasan bequeathed to him the staff of Shaykh Aḥmad al-Tijānī and one of the original copies of the *Jawāhir al-maʿānī*, written by the hand of ʿAlī Ḥarāzim and kept in the possession of al-Tijānī in Fez for sixteen years, which Shaykh Ḥasan had himself inherited from his father and Shaykh Ibrāhīm before him.

Shaykh al-Tijānī edited and published several important works, including Shaykh Ibrāhīm's magnum opus, *Kāshif al-ilbās* ("The Removal of Confusion"), and an edited collection of Shaykh Ibrāhīm's writings, which he named *Saʿādat al-anām* ("The Happiness of Humanity"). He also aided in the publication of a comprehensive collection of Shaykh Ibrāhīm's supplications, *Kanz al-Maṣūn* ("The Guarded Treasure"). Most recently, he has edited and published the aforementioned *Jawāhir al-maʿānī* based on the original bequeathed manuscript currently in his possession. Such invaluable work has not gone unnoticed. One Azhar scholar reportedly told

18 Shaykh al-Tijani Cissé, interview with Zachary Wright, Medina-Kaolack, June 2016.

him that his work identifying and analyzing *ḥadīth* citations in the 2001 publication of *Kāshif al-ilbās* would have been enough to earn him a doctoral degree at Azhar University. In the introduction to Shaykh al-Tijānī's publication of the *Kāshif*, Shaykh Ḥasan Cissé wrote: "I thank my dear brother, the master, the Shaykh, al-Tijānī ʿAlī Cissé, who spent of his efforts for the success of this pious work and much appreciated endeavor."

Shaykh al-Tijānī Cissé's own teachings span all fields of Islamic learning, from Prophetic traditions (*ḥadīth*), Islamic law, theology, and Sufism. During the month of Ramadan and on other occasions, he regularly teaches *ḥadīth* in the grand mosque following the early afternoon prayer (*ṣalāt al-ẓuhr*). He is fond of discussing minute details of Islamic law, and on one occasion I witnessed him evaluating the comparative strengths of various commentaries on the *Mukhtaṣar Sīdī Khalīl*, books he studied in Cairo, with a student of Mālikī jurisprudence. A significant concern for him is to remind Muslims of the correct prayer times – especially to seek the preferred time of the prayer (*al-waqt al-mukhtār*) above the mandated time (*al-ḍarūrī*) according to the Mālikī school – and to urge local sighting of the moon to determine the beginning of the lunar month.

The Shaykh's capacity to guide aspirants to the knowledge of God is oft attested to by disciples, who relate that his training (*tarbiya*) is gentle but focused.[19] Once on being asked about the manifestation of divine presences, he simply said, "When God has opened your eyes, just look, and you will find His realities everywhere." As for elaborate philosophizing about the divine emanations, he reminds aspirants that divine manifestations cannot be fixed into particular forms and are essentially beyond the confines of words: "All of that is misguidance," he said about the ideologization and fossilization of gnostic understandings. The Shaykh emphasizes the continued importance of personal connection to the living master for the transmission of gnosis (*maʿrifa*), or the knowledge of God. He ordinarily refuses to speak about the experience of gnosis in public settings, explaining: "It used to be that when the

---

19 Information in this paragraph derives from several interviews with disciples and the Shaykh in Medina-Baye, Kaolack, from September 2008 to July 2009.

shaykh and disciple sat together to discuss the knowledge of God, they would close the door as if they were thieves discussing their heist. But now people talk about this in the street." In any case, since gnosis is a gift from God bestowed on the servant, the aspirant's primary preoccupation should be in cultivating love for God, His Messenger, and the shaykh. He is thus fond of citing the words of Muḥammad al-Mishrī, the prominent Mauritanian disciple of Shaykh Ibrāhīm Niasse: "One kilo of love is better than three kilos of *ma'rifa*."[20] In practice, the sign of true knowledge of God thus manifests itself in love and emulation of the Prophet Muḥammad. This appears to be the reason, as evidenced in the speeches included in this volume, that the Shaykh exerts such effort in explaining the fundamentals of Islamic etiquette and understanding. When asked about the benefit of the Tijāniyya, he once told an Arab student in Morocco, "What we want from the Sufi path (*ṭarīqa*) is just to become better Muslims."

Aside from the lectures included in this volume, Shaykh al-Tijānī has also written a number of other sermons and speeches, in both Arabic and Wolofal (Wolof transliterated in Arabic script), as well as Arabic poetry. Among his poetry in praise of the Prophet, the following lines testify to his love for the "best of creation":

> O best of creation (*sayyid al-wujūd*), O fountainhead of the secret
>   O endower of lights, secretly and openly
> O manifestation of the truth, whose advent
>   Turned back the darkness of polytheism, never to return
> Surely you are the unseen of the Unseen, though many denied your mission
>   You bore testimony of another, of whom you are the manifest appearance
> If not for you, the Unseen would have remained so, without witness
>   If not for you, the Hidden would have remained concealed and secret

---

20 This statement appears to mirror that of the early Sufi Yaḥyā b. Mu'ādh, who said, "A mustard seed's worth of love, in my opinion, is better than seventy years of worship without love." See Alexander Knysh, *al-Qushayri's Epistle on Sufism* (Reading, UK: Garnet Publishing, 2007), 333.

Praise to God, after praise by his praise
    And by this praise, I became confirmed in my journey
And I preceded all others in all lands
    Though by no virtue of mine, O custodian of my treasure
O master, I am naught but a humble beggar at your door
    And I will never turn to another besides you...

Among the papers in his personal archive are a number of prayers written in his own handwriting that also demonstrate his love for the Prophet Muḥammad. Here is a prayer on the Prophet he wrote in a beautiful rhyme, each line ending in the sound *-āq*:

> O Allah, grant blessing and peace on the flashing light, whom You granted authority on the horizons, whom you honored with the winged horse (*al-burāq*), our master Muḥammad. May this prayer make us among the covenanted, and distance us from polytheism (*shirk*), doubt, hypocrisy, poverty, constriction, and destitution. And by it may we be honored by an abundance of provision. And upon his family and companions, may this prayer be multiplied by the number of the trees and leaves belonging to Allah.

The accompanying description relates that the Shaykh received this prayer by divine inspiration (*wāridāt*). Of course, Muslim saints (*awliyā'*) of the past are famous for their unveiling and reception of special prayers; and similar occurrences are recorded in reference to Shaykh Ibrāhīm, Sayyidī ʿAlī, and Shaykh Ḥasan Cissé. While some might use these events to justify the foundation of a new Sufi community (*ṭarīqa*), the many unveiled Tijānī shaykhs appear to integrate these unveilings within the existing framework of the Tijāniyya, thereby emphasizing that the foundation of a Sufi order is only by the direct command of the Prophet, not by the occurrence of the vision itself. Once Shaykh al-Tijānī Cissé was asked, "On whose authority do you speak? Do you see the Prophet?" The Shaykh responded, "To see the Prophet one or two times is not difficult. What is difficult is to be in a state where the Prophet is always with you." The petitioner insisted, "And is the Prophet always with you?" The Shaykh said quietly, "Indeed, the Prophet is never absent from me."[21] The Shaykh thus attested to his own inheritance from Shaykh Aḥmad al-Tijānī, who emphasized his path's potential to actualize an enduring connection to the spirituality of the Prophet Muḥammad.[22]

Shaykh al-Tijānī Cissé's connection to his namesake, Aḥmad al-Tijānī, appears attested by his grandfather Ibrāhīm Niasse often addressing him with the same epithet, "father of the flood" (*abū l-fayḍ*), used for the Tijāniyya's founder.[23] For his part, al-Tijānī Cissé has made several pious visitations (sing: *ziyāra*) to the tomb of Shaykh al-Tijānī in Fez, Morocco. On one such visit in 2004, he authored a poem with the following preface: "I was inspired with these verses during my *ziyāra* to our patron and master, the Imam and owner of this *Ṭarīqa Tijāniyya*, Shaykh Aḥmad b. Maḥammad al-Tijānī. I wrote them down and read them before the Shaykh, may God be pleased with him, as a means of rendering him homage and seeking intercession by him. I ask God the praised and exalted for acceptance." Here is the poem:

I offer my salutations to Ahmad al-Tijani
    Greetings by which I hope to quickly obtain my aspiration
O Ahmad, you are the one who quenches the creation's thirst by his secret
    You are the fountainhead of secrets in every divine presence (*ḥaḍra*)
The ocean of knowledge, guidance, and devotion
    The sprouting field of gnosis (*ʿirfān*), illumination (*nūr*), and wisdom (*ḥikma*)
The source of the flood (*abū l-fayḍ*) and of all goodness. Here I am at your door.
    Long before this day, was I covenanted in love

21 Dialogue between Shaykh al-Tijānī Cissé and Arab disciple in Morocco, witnessed by Zachary Wright, Rabat, Morocco, March, 2017.

22 Wright, *Realizing Islam: the Tijāniyya in North Africa and the Eighteenth-Century Muslim World* (UNC Press, 2020), 100-141.

23 Al-Tijānī b. ʿAlī Cissé, interview with Zachary Wright, Medina Baye Kaolack, Senegal, May 2016.

So (may God grant me) security, perfect faith, provision, and good health
Along with many children, and a long life
And pour forth (all goodness) in like manner, indeed I am certain
Of obtaining my request and goal
I direct myself to the Generous Lord by your blessing
And I ask that He heal my (maternal) uncles, my mother, and my brothers
And that He keep with us the secret of the inheritance (*sirr al-khilāfa*) for ever more
By the blessing of Abū Isḥāq (Ibrāhīm Niasse), my shaykh and support (*ʿumda*)
Blessings from the Most Merciful, continuously and forever
On the (Prophet Muḥammad) locus of secrets, the treasure of humanity
And on his family and companions, (a blessing enacted) whenever the speaker says
I offer my salutations to Ahmad al-Tijani.[24]

Notable in these verses is the attestation to Shaykh al-Tijānī's position as the "Seal of Saints" and "Hidden Pole", except from whose "ocean" of spiritual reality "no saint drinks or gives to drink" (see the following discourse on the "Seal of Saints" in this volume). Also of note is the emphasis on the claim of Shaykh Ibrāhīm Niasse and his spiritual successors to possess the fullest claim to the "secret" of the inheritance or authority (*sirr al-khilāfa*) within the Tijāniyya. From the perspective of his students, there is no doubt then that al-Tijānī Cissé, as the Imam of the community of Ibrāhīm Niasse, possesses the most comprehensive claim to overall leadership of the Tijāniyya Sufi order.

The scholarship and humanitarian mission of Shaykh al-Tijānī Cissé have been recognized by several government and international bodies. The Senegalese government appointed him as Senegal's General

24 I thank Shaykh al-Tijānī Cissé for providing me a copy of this poem, dated Friday, 19 Jumādī al-Thāniya 1425 (6 August 2004).

Commissioner for the Hajj in 2001. In 2006, he was again recognized by former Senegalese President Abdoulaye Wade and appointed a Senegalese "Special Missions Ambassador." He has also received Senegal's distinguished award, the *Ordre de Merite* (1993). On a recent trip to Atlanta, Georgia (January 2011), he received the city's prestigious Phoenix Award. Beginning in 2013, successive reports issued by Jordan's Royal Islamic Strategic Studies Centre and Georgetown University's Center for Muslim-Christian Understanding have ranked Shaykh al-Tijānī among the top twenty-five of the world's "500 most influential Muslims."

This collection contains the Imam's speeches delivered between 2011 and 2018 in various countries around the world, including the United Kingdom, Germany, the United States, Ivory Coast, Ghana, and Burkina Faso. For most of these speeches, I served as the live translator while the Imam spoke. Often, the Arabic text that the Imam provided me in advance was much longer than the words he delivered on stage. This collection tries to reflect the discourses as delivered in preference to the written text. In a few places, this redaction joins speeches together on a similar subject; and greetings and gratitude expressed specific to the place of deliverance are frequently omitted. For legibility, also frequently omitted are the customary "God's blessing and peace upon him" after mention of the Prophet Muḥammad. Most of the Qur'ān verses mentioned have been identified, but many of the *ḥadīth* have been left unsourced. In some cases, I have inserted or altered subtitles from the original Arabic script, and in some instances I have inserted connecting sentences in parentheses to facilitate comprehension. We look forward to the publication of collected Arabic speeches of Shaykh al-Tijānī Cissé in the near future. This translation is an excerpted selection of this more significant corpus. The reader is nonetheless assured that every word included in this volume was at one point delivered by the Imam to a live audience.

1.

Peace, Tolerance, and Moderation in Islam

Lectures presented in Atlanta, USA (2011); Ouagadougou, Burkina Faso (2011); London, UK (2016); Bonn, Germany (2016)

In the Name of God, the Beneficent, the Merciful

Praise to God, praiseworthy in His Essence, in His Attributes, in His Names. He it was who honored humankind with His blessing, His benevolence, and His grace. The Most High said, "*We have honored the children of Adam; provided them with transportation on land and sea; given them for sustenance things good and pure; and conferred upon them special favors above a great part of Our creation.*"[25]

And may the peace and blessing of God be upon the perfect human being (*al-insān al-kāmil*), the mercy of God to all (*raḥmat Allāh al-shāmil*), our master Muḥammad. He it was who firmly fixed the laws of this community of security, that whoever should put them into practice would be a Muslim and would live in peace. Such a person will treat others with peace, and he will carry to all the message of peace.

Indeed, the Prophet was he who commanded us with beauty in all things, and beautiful behavior to all created beings. He informed us of a woman who was damned for mistreating a cat. She refused to feed it, nor would she let it go to eat from the sustenance of the earth. If this is the case for a cat, what of the one who mistreats a human being?

And may God's blessing and peace also be on the family of the Prophet, upon his companions, and upon all those of his community who follow them in righteousness until the Day of Judgment.

Your Excellencies: eminent ambassadors, ministers, counselors; respected doctors, professors, scholars; distinguished imams, shaykhs, and Muslim brethren, each one of you according to your name and title – I greet you with the most beautiful and pure words: "Peace to you and mercy and blessing of God Most High."

It is with a heart full of happiness that I find myself among you today to speak on a subject of great importance to all of us: "Islam and Peace." Especially in these later times, some find recourse in blind accusations against Islam, linking it to violence, and other things of which the religion is innocent. In the following brief exposition, we intend to demonstrate based on well-established evidence, that Islam is a religion

---

25 Qur'ān, 17:70.

of virtue and conciliation toward the whole of the human race. And in this we seek the help of God the Most High.

Peace in Islam

Peace is certainly one of the basic principles that Islam has rooted deeply in the souls of Muslims. It has thus become fused to their very beings, and it is certainly an integral doctrine among their beliefs. The name for this religion – *al-Islām* – is derived from the word *salām*, "peace." This is because peace and Islam are mutually supportive, constituent elements in providing serenity, security, and tranquility. One of the names of God, glorious and exalted is He, is the name, "The Peace." Indeed, it is God who provides security to humanity in what He has legislated among the foundational principles, and in what He has delineated by way of proscriptions and procedures. Consequently, the one who bears this message of Islam is the one who bears the banner of peace, for he brings to humankind direction, light, goodness, and guidance.

Peace is the greeting of the Muslims, a greeting that reconciles hearts, strengthens bonds, and joins man to his brother man. The generous extension and establishment of peace throughout the world is a component of faith itself. Thus did God make this enunciation of peace the greeting of the Muslims, reminding them that their religion is a religion of peace and security, that they are the people of serenity and the lovers of peace. The Messenger of God said, "God has made peace a greeting for our community, and a reliable trust for the people under the protection of the Muslims (*ahl al-dhimma*)."[26]

A person should not even speak to another person until he has begun with the greetings of peace. As the Messenger of Islam said, "Greetings of peace should precede any conversation."[27] The reason for this is that Islam is a guarantee of safety, and there can be no conversation unless safety is assured.

---

26 Ḥadīth in al-Ṭabarānī, *Muʿjam al-kabīr*.

27 Ḥadīth in al-Tirmidhī, *al-Sunan*.

The Muslim is entrusted – and this is a secret entrusted to him by his Lord – with sending greetings of peace on his Prophet, on himself, and on the righteous servants of God.

As for the sphere of war and battle, if the word of peace should be pronounced on the tongue of the enemy combatant, it is incumbent to stop fighting him. The Most High said, "*When you go out (to fight) in the cause of God, do not say to the one who offers you the greeting of peace, 'You are not a believer.'*"[28]

God's greeting to the believers on the Day of Judgment is also "Peace." The Most High said, "*Their greeting on the Day when they meet Him will be 'Peace.'*"[29] And He, majestic is His affair, also said: "*'Peace' – a word (of salutation) from a Merciful Lord.*"[30] The greetings of the Angels to the human beings in Paradise will be "Peace." "*And the Angels shall enter unto them from every gate, saying, 'Peace be to you.'*"[31] There the residence of the righteous will be the abode of security and peace: "*God does invite to the abode of peace.*"[32] And He said, "*For them is the abode of peace in the presence of their Lord.*"[33]

The word "peace" comes in the Qur'ān forty-six times, and it comes in the specific form of the greeting ten times. Together this makes fifty-six times in fifty verses from twenty-eight chapters of the Qur'ān. This is just an indication of the pre-eternal importance of peace with the Lord of Islam. By way of comparison, the word "war" is mentioned in the noble Qur'ān only six times.

If this is Islam, who then is the Muslim? The best definition of the Muslim is that presented by the Messenger of God when he said, "The Muslim is the one who grants others safety from his tongue and hand, and the Emigrant (*muhājir*) is the one who emigrates from what God has prohibited him."[34]

---

28 Qur'ān, 4:94. By offering the greeting of peace in this case, the combatant would be demonstrating his conversion to Islam.

29 Qur'ān, 33:44.

30 Qur'ān, 36:58.

31 Qur'ān, 13:23-4.

32 Qur'ān, 10:25.

33 Qur'ān, 6:127.

34 Ḥadīth in al-Bukhārī, Ṣaḥīḥ.

The Tolerance and Ease of Islam

The sacred law of Islam in its entirety – for those who accept it, trust in it, and observe it – is a blessing, mercy, justice, and benefit to human beings in this life and the next. The Prophet, God's blessing and peace on him, said, "The most beloved of religions to God is that which is true (*ḥanīf*) and tolerant (*samḥa*)." Thus did God, glorious and exalted is He, send the Prophet with truth and tolerance to liberate humanity from its burdens and shackles, as was the state of the nations before us whenever punishment befell them. The Most High said, "*He (the Messenger) releases them from their heavy burden and the shackles that were on them.*"[35] Indeed, God has lightened the constriction (*ḥaraj*) upon this community in terms of what He commanded and prohibited us. "*He has not made the religion constricted for you.*"[36] In this way, our Lord informs us that He desires ease for us in what He has legislated for us, "*God desires ease for you, not hardship.*"[37] If a Muslim truly reflects on this sacred law, he will see the tolerance and ease readily apparent in the commands and prohibitions. "*The word of your Lord has been perfected in truth and justice. None can change His words. And He is the All-Hearing, the All-Knowing.*"[38]

Let us look at the basic foundation of this religion, which is the Oneness (*tawḥīd*) of the Lord of the worlds, and the sincerity in religion owed to Him. When the Muslims were severely tried in Mecca, when the weak and those without protectors were tormented, when they were persecuted and insulted, God said to them, "*(Judgment is upon) the one who apostatizes after having accepted the faith, except under compulsion with his heart remaining firm in the faith.*"[39] So it was even permitted for them to pronounce the words of infidelity as a means of delivering themselves from the torment, oppression and enmity of the idolaters.

---

35 Qur'ān, 7:157.

36 Qur'ān, 22:78.

37 Qur'ān, 2:185.

38 Qur'ān, 6:115.

39 Qur'ān, 16:106.

Let us also look at the legal obligations (*farā'iḍ*) of Islam. God made ritual purity (*ṭahāra*) a condition for performing the prayer, as in the Prophetic narration: "God does not accept the prayer without ritual purification." Even though purity is a condition for performing the prayer, the Muslim is permitted the dispensation of attaining ritual purity with clean earth (*tayammum*),[40] when there is no water present, or when he is cannot use water (for purification) due to sickness, open wounds or the like. As God said, "*If you find not water, then cleanse yourselves with clean earth.*"[41] And in the Prophet's words, "The earth was made a place of prayer for me, and a source of purity."[42]

God made it obligatory in the ritual prayer - which is the second pillar of Islam - to stand, bow, prostrate, and to face the direction of the sacred house in Mecca. But these obligations are lifted from the one who is unable to perform them. The Prophet said, "Pray standing, or sitting down if you are unable to stand, or laying down on your side if you are unable to sit." Thus, the Muslim prays according to his capacity. God says, "*If you are in fear, pray on foot or while riding.*"[43] And this is the case for the one facing Mecca or the one not facing it, if the latter should have a valid reason for that.

It is also an aspect of Islam's ease and tolerance that, should a Muslim intend to do good, but be unable to do it, God rewards him according to his intention. The Prophet said, "If a servant is sick or on a journey, God writes for him what he would have done if he was healthy or present."

If we were to recount all the instances of Islam's ease and tolerance in the realm of ritual worship, the discussion would become long indeed. But these representative statements, little as they are, should suffice by way of indication and proof.

---

40 *Tayammum* is ritual purification performed with clean earth (sand, stone, etc.) instead of water.

41 Qur'ān, 4:43.

42 Ḥadīth in al-Bukhārī, *Ṣaḥīḥ*. The narration continues, "therefore let my community pray wherever they are when the prayer is due."

43 Qur'ān, 2:239.

The Tolerance of Islam for Non-Muslims

Islam's tolerance for non-Muslims is an established and legislated reality, as well as a fundamental trait of the Islamic character. This trait has been exemplified in the noble Qur'ān, in the authentic Prophetic norm (*sunna*), by the righteously guided successors of the Prophet, and by the Muslim community that followed them. History is the best witness to this. Tolerance with non-Muslims manifested in numerous ways and forms. Among these is that Islam acknowledges the religions of the non-Muslims, with the condition that they submit to the political sovereignty of the Muslims (when abiding in the Islamic state).

Muslims are also permitted to eat meat killed by Jews and Christians (*ahl al-kitāb*), so long as it is not sacrificed for other than God. Muslim men are also permitted to marry the virtuous women among them. God said, "*This day have all good things been made lawful for you. The food of those who have received the Scripture is lawful for you, and your food is lawful for them. And (lawful to you) are the virtuous women of the believers and the virtuous women of those who received the Scripture before you, when you give them their due dowers and live with them in honor, not in fornication, nor taking them as secret concubines.*"[44]

Islam encourages justice with the non-Muslims and acting in the best of ways towards them. The Most High said, "*God does not forbid you, with regard to those who did not fight you on account of religion and did not expel you from your homes, from dealing kindly and justly with them. For God loves those who are just.*"[45]

Islam also allows the non-Muslims (living under Muslim rule) to keep their houses of worship, to repair those sites that have fallen into ruin, and to rebuild what has been pulled down (by miscreants). God said, "*Had not God repelled some men by means of other men, the monasteries, churches, synagogues, and mosques – in which the Name of God is celebrated abundantly – would surely have been pulled down.*"[46]

---

44 Qur'ān, 5:5.

45 Qur'ān, 60:8.

46 Qur'ān, 22:40.

These are just some instances in which Islam's tolerance towards non-Muslims is apparent.

The Tolerance of the Prophet and his working together with non-Muslims

God Most High sent His Prophet Muḥammad as a mercy to all the worlds, and he is an exemplar of human perfection in all aspects of his life. He is an exemplar of perfection in his relationship with his Lord, and in his relationship with all people, whatever their gender, age, color, or religion. Jābir b. ʿAbdallāh, may God be pleased with him, said: "The Messenger of God was an easy-going man." Al-Nawawī explained, "This means gentleness of disposition, with nobility in each aspect of his character. He was possessed of a character that was gracious and easy-going." According to the authentic statement of ʿĀʾisha, may God be pleased with her: "The Messenger of God never chose between two things except that he chose the easiest of them, unless it was a sin, in which case he would be farthest of people from it. The Messenger of God did not seek redress on his own behalf, except if the sanctity of God were transgressed, then he would seek redress for the sake of God."

Such were the values to which the Prophet called: ease in all things, together with defense of God's sacred rights, but not for worldly show or egotistical passions. The biography of the Prophet contains numerous examples of this tolerance with non-Muslims. Although this subject is boundless, I will just mention a few examples:

As mentioned above, the Prophet was a mercy to whole of creation, for it was he about whom God said, *"And We have not sent you except as a mercy to all the worlds."*[47] He was thus a mercy presented to the entire creation. And he encouraged affection and mercy among humankind. He said: "God has no mercy on the one who has no mercy for humankind." And the word "humankind" (*al-nās*) here includes every single individual among humankind, whatever gender or religion.

47 Qur'ān, 21:107.

There are many examples of this mercy in the foundational texts. In (the *ḥadīth* collection of) al-Bukhārī, we find the following narration from the Prophet in the chapter concerning mercy to humankind and animals: "For any Muslim who grows a plant: should another person or animal come to eat from that plant, it will count as charity (*ṣadaqa*) for him." The religion of Islam is thus a religion of tolerance and mercy that encompasses the entirety of humankind, surrounding all of them in mercy and righteousness.

The Prophet pardoned those who fought against him or showed him enmity. His magnanimity on the day of the Muslims' conquest of Mecca represented the height of forgiveness ever reached by a human being, for he forgave his enemies. His position towards those who had been at war with the mission of Islam, and who had never put down their swords, was far from exacting revenge upon them, for he told them, "Go, for you are free!"

The Prophet prayed for those who turned against him from among the non-Muslims. Once al-Ṭufayl b. ʿAmrū al-Dawsī and his companions[48] presented themselves to the Prophet and said, "O Messenger of God, the Daws people have rejected Islam and turned away, so pray to God against them!" When the Prophet raised his hands, they said, "May the Daws be destroyed," thinking that he was praying against them. But he said, "O God! Guide the people of Daws and bring them to Islam."

The Prophet also commanded the joining of familial relations, even if one's family members are not Muslims. He said to Asmāʾ, the daughter of Abū Bakr, "Keep up relations with your (non-Muslim) mother."[49]

---

48 Al-Ṭufayl was the leader of the Daws people in the village of Tihama (southern Arabia). He converted to Islam and brought eighty families of Muslim converts from his people to complain to the Prophet about the rest of the Daws people. The Daws later embraced Islam in their entirety.

49 The mother of Asmāʾ, named Qutayla, had been divorced from Abū Bakr in pre-Islamic times and was not a Muslim. When Qutayla came to visit Asmāʾ in Medina, she at first refused to receive her mother until ordered to do so by the Prophet. This was also the occasion for the revelation of the verse previously mentioned, "God forbids you not ... from dealing kindly and justly with them" (60:8).

The tolerance of Muslims after the Prophet in dealing with the non-Muslims

Abū Bakr, may God be pleased with him, used to advise the Muslim armies by saying, "You will come across a people cloistered in monasteries, claiming they are so for the sake of God. Leave them alone, and do not destroy their monasteries." His successor, ʿUmar, may God be pleased with him, used to admonish Muslims to fulfill their pledge to those under their protection (*ahl al-dhimma*): that they should defend them against those who threatened them, and that they should not demand too much of them.

ʿUmar b. al-Khaṭṭāb once passed by a gate in which an old blind man was begging. He put his hand on the man's arm and asked, "Are you Jewish or Christian?" The man said, "I am Jewish." He asked, "And what has brought you to this misfortune?" The man said, "The tax on protected non-Muslims (*jizya*), needs, and old age." So ʿUmar took him by the hand and went with him to his house, gave him a gift, and then went with him to the keeper of the treasury. He said, "Look at this man and those like him! By God, we have not been just with him, having taken from him in his youth and then failed him in his old age. '*Alms are for the poor and needy*.'[50] The poor (*fuqarāʾ*) are among the Muslims, and this man is among the needy (*masākīn*) from the People of the Book." Then he returned to him and those like him the protective tax (*jizya*).

In fact, the fair dealing of the Muslims with others was one of the principal reasons that many people entered Islam. They found in Islam tolerance and fraternity between different groups of people (*shuʿūb*), and no preference for one race or descent group over another, except in a person's capacity in adhering to the religion in both word and deed. Nothing other than this caused their adherence.

The Messenger of God said: "The one who does injustice to a covenanted party (*muʿāhid*), or who deprives him of his right, or demands something beyond his capacity, or takes from him something that does not belong to him, will have to argue with me on the Day of Judgment." And he said, "The one who kills a covenanted person will not smell the fragrance of Paradise, even if the scent traveled a distance of forty years."

50 Qur'ān, 9:60.

Imam al-Bukhārī mentioned in his *Ṣaḥīḥ* that the Caliph ʿUmar b. al-Khaṭṭāb, may God be pleased with him, said, "I advise you all to uphold the promise to the protected peoples (*dhimma*), for they are the protected ones of your Prophet, and blessing (*rizq*) for your families." It has likewise been reported that ʿUmar returned the protective tax (*jizya*) to the Christians of Muʾtah when the Muslims felt they would be unable to defend them against the Romans.

Islam rejects fanaticism

There are many textual proofs concerning the ease (*yusr*) of Islam. I will briefly mention some of general narrations speaking about tolerance and ease in the religion.

As reported by Abū Umāma, may God be pleased with him: "The wife of ʿUthmān b. Maẓʿūn was a beautiful, fragrant woman, who loved to adorn and groom herself for her husband. Once ʿĀʾisha came to visit her and found her disheveled and unkempt. She asked her, 'What is wrong with you?' She responded, 'A group of the Companions of the God's Messenger have isolated themselves for the sake of worship. Among them are ʿAlī b. Abī Ṭālib, ʿAbdallāh b. Rawāḥa, and ʿUthmān b. Maẓʿūn. They forbade themselves from women and from eating meat. They fast the days and pray all night. I was afraid that I might tempt him with the state (of adornment) I was in, calling him away from what he had intended.' When the Prophet came home and ʿĀʾisha informed him of this, he went to them straight away, barely grabbing his sandals with his left index finger. When he found them, he asked what they were doing. They said, 'We were seeking blessing (*khayr*).' Then God's Messenger said: 'I have surely been sent with the true, tolerant religion; I have not been sent with the monasticism innovated by men. For surely there were peoples who invented monasticism, then it became decreed for them, and then they were unable to perform it properly. Eat meat and go to your wives. Fast and then break your fast. Pray and then sleep. For such have I been commanded.'"[51]

51 Ḥadīth found in Aḥmad b. Ḥanbal, *Musnad*.Ḥ

Ibn ʿAbbās related that God's Messenger said in a sermon: "God, Mighty and Majestic is He, gave rights to each one to whom a right is due. He made the obligations obligatory. He issued proscriptions, and He delimited the penalties. He made the lawful things lawful, and He made the prohibited things prohibited. He set the laws of the religion, and He made this an easy and tolerant religion. He made it inclusive (*wāsiʿ*), he did not make it restrictive."

Ibn al-Adraʿ narrated: "I was guarding the Prophet one night, and he came out to do something. He saw me and took me by the hand, and we proceeded on our way together. We passed by a man who was praying, reciting the Qurʾān in a loud voice. The Prophet said, 'He is just trying to be seen.' I said, 'O Messenger of God, he is just reciting the Qurʾān loudly in his prayer.' He let go of my hand, then said, 'None of you will obtain the goodness of this matter through exaggeration.' I was on guard another night when he came out for something. He took me by the hand and passed by another man reciting the Qurʾān (normally) in his prayer. I said, 'He is just trying to be seen.' But the Prophet said, 'No, in fact he is a pious man.' Then I looked, and saw it was ʿAbdallāh dhū al-Nijādayn (of the two sword-belts)."[52]

Moderation (*wasaṭiyya*) in Islam

Praise to God, who said in His clear book: *"Surely We have made you a moderate community, so that you may be a witness over mankind, and that the Messenger may be a witness over you."* (2:143). Moderation is the reason behind this community's selection as the best brought forth for mankind.

The meaning of "moderate" (*wasaṭ*) here is the most just course, the way of goodness and excellence, as well as the middle way between two opposites. Such an understanding makes clear that Islam is a religion of moderation, neither tending towards fanatical extremism nor unbridled distortion. The people of wisdom have said: "Every praiseworthy virtue has two blameworthy extremes." Generosity is thus the middle path

52 Narration in Aḥmad b. Ḥanbal, *Musnad*.

between stinginess and squandering, and bravery is the middle course between cowardliness and recklessness.

God the Most High has described His religion and sacred law in comparison to others as the balanced path, for He the Glorified said, "*Verily, this is My straight path, so follow it. Do not follow other ways for they will sever you from His way. This has He commanded you, so that you may be reverent.*"[53] Indeed, God described Himself, exalted is His affair, as being on a straight path, for He said, "*Verily my Lord is on a straight path.*"[54]

Islam calls for moderation and it denounces extremism, distortion, and departing from the middle of the road. God, the Mighty and Majestic, characterizes those who lack self-restraint in their religion as being on brink of ruin (*ḥarf*). The Most High said, "*Among mankind is one who worships God on the brink: if good befalls him, he is content; but if a trial comes to him, he falls on his face, losing this world and next. And that is an obvious loss.*"[55]

We find balanced moderation in everything about which the Qur'ān speaks. The complete meaning of balance is readily evident in the Qur'ān's juxtaposition of the ephemeral world and the Afterlife; of reward and punishment; of the soul (*nafs*), the spirit (*rūḥ*), and the body; of the heavens and the earth; of the night and the day; of fear and hope; of contemplation and action; of good and evil; of justice (ʿadl) and preference (*faḍl*). And this is found throughout the Qur'ān.

The word "middle" (*wasaṭ*) derives its meaning from being between, or disengaged from, two blameworthy extremes. But there is no such blessed middle between something praiseworthy and blameworthy. You cannot commend something by saying, "That is the middle between goodness and wickedness" or "between beauty and ugliness."

The middle way is the most choice, select way; for the middle of the river valley (*wādī*) is best place in the valley. It is said that a person is the "middle (or center) of his people" when his lineage is the most well established and when his honor is most venerated. Among the description of our Prophet, God's blessing and peace upon him, is that he was the "center of his people",

53 Qur'ān, 6:153.

54 Qur'ān, 11:56.

55 Qur'ān, 22:11.

meaning the "best of them." God made the Prophet's community the middle community, thus the best. Indeed, the middle or center is the best or most exalted of something, for the center of each thing is its point of balance. The source of this (understanding) is that the best of something is found at its middle point, for excess and shortcoming are both blameworthy.

According to Zamakhsharī:[56] "It is said that the best belongs to the middle, for the extremes are plunged in imbalance, and the middle course is guarded and protected. Concerning this Abū Tamām said:

'She was the protected center, and what surrounded her
Of (momentous) occurrences did not push her to the edge.'"

God said, *"Like this we made you a moderate community."*[57] In other words: forbearing and (divinely) selected. Similar are the words of the Most High: *"The most moderate of them said, 'Did I not tell you to praise (your Lord)?'"*[58] The word "moderate" here clearly means "the best and most just of them."

Surely it is from God's wisdom that He chose moderation as the distinguishing characteristic of this last religious community, for this revelation that sealed all (previous) divine revelations, and for the seal of prophets sent as the messenger to all mankind and as a mercy to all the worlds.

In Islam, the goal of taking up the middle position is for the Muslim to strive for moderation and distance himself from extremism in words or deeds. This is so that he does not go beyond the bounds, nor come up short. He is neither neglectful nor excessive, for both negligence and excess are blameworthy. God has prohibited both extremes and reproached both the neglectful and the exaggerators. The Most High said, *"Be steadfast as you were commanded, along with those who repent with you, and do not exceed the limits."*[59] Moderation and balance agree with the natural disposition of humankind. Human beings have been created weak, afflicted with languor

---

56 Maḥmūd b. ʿUmar al-Zamakhsharī (d. 1144) was a Persian theologian and commentator on the Qurʾān.

57 Qurʾān, 2:143.

58 Qurʾān, 68:28.

59 Qurʾān, 11:112.

and laziness, and subjected to work. They alternate between strength and weakness, health and sickness. Thus, balance is appropriate to them, harmonizing their states. Surely an exalted (spiritual) aspiration and strength are best for a person: but should one incline towards severity, he is returned to incapacity, and his (spiritual) journey is obstructed. This Muslim community is thus a community of moderation in every sense of the word.

Both the sacred law and reason call for moderation and balance. According to the statement of the Prophet in *(Ṣaḥīḥ) al-Bukhārī*: "Surely religion is ease, and no one makes it difficult except that it overpowers him. So maintain the middle course, and attain proximity (to the divine)."[60] According to another narration, "Moderation! Content yourselves with moderation (*qisṭ*)."[61]

According to Ibn ʿAbbās, "The Messenger of God, the peace and blessing of God upon him, asked me on the day of ʿAqaba while he was on his camel, 'Pick up some pebbles for me.' So, I picked up some stones the size of those used in a slingshot. When I put them in his hand he said, '(Yes) like these. Beware of exaggeration in religion, surely those before you were destroyed for exaggerating in their religion.'"[62]

The Prophet, God's blessing and peace upon him, once gave the following example. According to Jābir b. ʿAbdallāh, "We were once with the Prophet, God's blessing and peace upon him. He drew one line (in the sand) and two other lines on the right and left of the first. Then he put his hand on the middle line and said, 'This is the way of God.' Then he recited the verse, '*This is My straight path, so follow it, and do not follow other ways, for you will be separated from His way.*'"[63]

There are many Qur'an verses and Prophetic sayings encouraging moderation and praising those who practice it. Islam provides Muslims a moderate way of life, between those who "*revel and eat as beasts*"[64] and those who "*forbid themselves the good things which God made lawful*

---

60 Ḥadīth on the authority of Abū Hurayra in Bukhārī and Muslim.

61 Ḥadīth in Ibn Majah, on authority of Jabir b. Abd-Allāh: "O people, you must be moderate, you must be moderate, you must be moderate. Verily God will not give up until you give up."

62 Ḥadīth in the Musnad of Imam Aḥmad, al-Nasāʾī and Ibn Majah.

63 Qurʾān, 6:153.

64 Qurʾān, 47:12.

for them."[65] God, exalted is His affair, said: "*O Children of Adam! Adorn yourselves at every place of prayer and eat and drink. But do not waste by excess, God loves not the wasteful. Say: 'Who has forbidden the beautiful gifts of God, which He has brought forth for His servants, and the good things of His providing?' Say, 'That is for the believers in this world, and on the Day of Judgment it will be for them alone.' Thus do we explain Our signs in detail for those who understand.*"[66] And the Most High said, "*O you who believe, do not prohibit the good things that God made lawful to you, and do not transgress. God does not like the transgressors. And eat of what God has provided, lawful and good. And fear God, in whom you believe.*"[67] In this way, Islam combines the goodness of this world with the goodness of the next, so that this world is a place of planting for the Hereafter. And in this way, Islam rejects fanaticism and the prohibition of beautiful and good things, just as it denounces the other extreme of preoccupation with self-indulgence and lustful desires.

Islam encourages moderation in applying the sacred law, for God the Most High said: "*If you carry out punishment, punish with the like of what you were afflicted. But if you patiently endure, verily that is a blessing for the patient.*"[68] We are also required to hold to moderation in our religious ideologies. The Most High said, "*O people of the Book! Do not commit excess in your religion, nor say of God other than the truth. The Messiah, Jesus, son of Mary, was (no more than) a Messenger of God, and His Word bestowed on Mary, and a spirit from Him. So believe in God and His messengers, and do not speak of a 'Trinity.' Cease: it will be better for you! God is only One God. Glorified is He above having a son. To Him belong all things in the heavens and on earth. And God suffices as a Trustee.*"[69] Such was the affair of Jesus, upon whom be peace: God the Glorified prohibited people from insulting Jesus by disparaging his station (*manzila*) or by raising him above his capacity.

The Most High encouraged moderation in expenditure, saying: "*And do not make your hand as chained to your neck, nor extend it completely,*

---

65 Qur'ān, 5:87.

66 Qur'ān, 7:31-32.

67 Quran, 5:87-88.

68 Qur'ān, 16:126.

69 Qur'ān, 4:171.

becoming either blamed or bereft."[70] And the Most High said: "*They are those who, when they spend, do so neither excessively nor sparingly, but in between, justly moderate.*"[71] (Islam also encourages moderation in affection and disaffection:) Abū Hurayra, may his fame be raised, reported: "Love your beloved (friend) with gentleness. Perhaps one day he will become loathsome to you. And let your dislike for those your loath be within limits. Perhaps one day he will become your beloved."[72]

The Prophet prohibited his companions from exaggeration in worship lest they should experience suffering. He said to his companions who wanted to deny themselves the good things of the world thinking that would bring them greater proximity to God: "By God, I am the most God-fearing and pious among you, but I fast, and then break my fast. I pray and then I rest. I marry women. Whoever has a distaste for my example (*sunna*), he is not from me." And the Most High said, "*God does not burden a soul beyond what it can bear. It gains every good that it earns and suffers every ill that it earns.*"[73] And He, exalted is His word, said: "*So reverence God as much as you can. Listen and obey. And spend in God's cause for the benefit of your own self. Whoever is saved from the miserliness of his own self, he is the successful one.*"[74] The Most High said, "*Call upon your Lord in humility and in secret. Surely He does not like the transgressors*"[75] And He said: "*And remember your Lord in humility and fear, silently within yourself, in the morning and evening. And do not be among the heedless.*"[76] And the Most High said, "*And do not recite your prayers too loudly or too quietly, but seek the middle way.*"[77]

According to Buraydat al-Aslamī, "I came out one day for something and encountered the Prophet, God's blessing and peace upon him. He walked with me for a while, and he took my hand and we proceeded

70 Qur'ān, 17:29.

71 Qur'ān, 25:67.

72 *Ḥadīth* in Tirmidhi.

73 Qur'ān, 2:286.

74 Qur'ān, 64:16.

75 Qur'ān, 7:55.

76 Qur'ān, 7:205.

77 Qur'ān, 17:110.

together until we came to a man praying with much bowing and prostration. The Prophet, God's blessing and peace upon him said, 'Do you see what is to be seen?' I said, 'God and His Messenger know best [what is to be seen].' He let go of my hand, clasped his hands, and then turned them upwards and repeated three times, 'Take up the guidance with moderation. Whoever makes this religion difficult will be vanquished by it.'"[78]

According to ʿAbdallāh b. ʿAmrū, "It was mentioned to the Messenger of God, God's blessing and peace upon him, that men were exerting themselves strenuously in worship. He said, "This is the appetite (*ḍarāwa*) of Islam and its youthful zeal (*shirra*). And for every appetite there is a zeal, and for every zeal there is a repose (*fatra*). Whoever finds repose in the middle course and in my *sunna* is blessed. Whoever finds repose in disobedience is destroyed."[79]

Miqdām b. Maʿdī Karib reported: "I heard the Messenger of God, God's blessing and peace upon him, say: 'The son of Adam has never filled a vessel more vile than his stomach, for a few bites is enough for him to keep his back straight. But if overcome by appetite, let him fill it a third with food, a third with drink, and a third with air to breath.'"[80]

Jābir b. Samura reported: "I used to pray with the Messenger of God, God's blessing and peace upon him. His prayer was to the point, and his sermon was to the point."

According to Anas b. Mālik, may God be pleased with him: "Three groups of people came to the houses of the Prophet's wives, God's blessing and peace upon him, and they asked about the worship of the Prophet, God's blessing and peace upon him. When they were told, it was as if they thought it was little, and then they said, 'Where are we in relation to the Messenger of God, God's blessing and peace upon him, who has been forgiven his past and future wrongs?' One of them said, 'I will pray all of every night.' Another said, 'I will fast every day and not eat.' Another said, 'I will withdraw from women and never marry.' The Messenger of God came out to them and said, 'Are you the ones who

78 Ḥadīth in the Musnad of Aḥmad and the Mustadrak of Tirmidhi.

79 Ḥadīth of similar wording found in the Musnad of Imam Aḥmad.

80 Ḥadīth in Ibn Majah.

have been saying these things? By God, I am the most God-fearing and pious among you, but I fast and eat, I pray and rest, and I marry women. Whoever disdains my example (*sunna*) has nothing to do with me.'"[81]

Ibn Masʿūd said, "Economized actions while following the *sunna* is better than strenuous exertion in performing innovations." Similarly, Ubayy b. Kaʿb said, "Stick to the path and the *sunna*, for surely the fire will not touch the servant on God's way and the *sunna*, who remembers the Merciful with eyes overflowing in fear of God. The middle course in God's way and the *sunna* is better than exertion in misguidance."

Moderation is surely among the special characteristics of this community. It is the reason for its benediction. The community's blessing will persist so long as it guards this distinguishing characteristic of moderation, which may also be likened to fairness and steadfastness on the path of God, exalted and majestic is He. If a community should depart from the middle to one side, falling into either negligence or excess, it will meet with ruin. Surely the extremes are places of destruction. And the extreme of excess and exaggeration is not distinguished from the extreme of negligence and shortcoming: both are places of ruin for either the individual or the society.

The one who is negligent and comes up short in upholding the right of God is an extremist, no different than the one who goes to extremes in the direction of excess and severity, making obligatory that which is not obligatory, or prohibiting that which is not prohibited.

It is these latter extremists today who declare Muslims to be infidels and righteous people to be corrupt. They make licit the shedding of blood, and the theft of peoples' property. They rebel against their governments and rulers. They stir up chaos and spread corruption on the earth. "*And they account themselves as those who do good work.*"[82]

To us has come the sound narration (from the Prophet): "This knowledge is born away from all who contravene the balance (*ʿudūl*),[83] and it is made an exile in the perversion of the fanatic, the presumption

---

81 Ḥadīth in Bukhari and Muslim.

82 Qur'ān, 18:104. The full verse reads: "*Those whose efforts are lost in the worldly life, and they account themselves as those who do good work.*"

83 Plural of ʿ*idl*, two halves of sack carried by beast of burden.

of the misguided liar, and in the interpretation of the ignorant."[84] The perversion of the fanatic is a reference to the extremist's bigotry (*taʿaṣṣub*) and severity. The presumption of the liar means an exaggerated opinion of one's intellectual capacity in matters of legislation. The presumption of the liar also means the pursuit of vain passion. The interpretation of the ignorant concerns ignorance of the sources of legal judgments (*aḥkām*) and the procedures of deriving understanding from these sources.

The meaning here is that the sublime teachings of Islam are far removed from the superficial misinterpretations of those only at the surface (of the religion). It is far removed from the stupidity of the ignorant. Islam is the divine, tolerant, and moderate religion. Its foundation is (the verse), "*Seek the abode of the hereafter through what God has given you, but do not forget your portion of the world. Do good as God has done good to you. And do not commit corruption in the earth, for God does not love the corrupters.*"[85]

The pursuit of selfish desires is the source of deviation from the God's straight path. God said, "*If they do not respond to you, know that they follow their (own) vain desires, and who is more misguided than the one follows his desire instead of guidance from God. Surely God does not guide the wrongdoers.*"[86]

And the Most High said, "*Have you not seen those who took their own desires as their god? So God misled them in (their) understanding, and sealed their ears and hearts, and put blinders over their eyes. So who can guide them after God (has misled them)? Be reminded!*"[87] It is well known that the pursuit of vain desires sweeps away all religion, kills all goodness, and is the herald of evil. It brings division, dissension, differentiation, controversy, enmity, disgust, hatred, disturbance, confusion, and turmoil.

---

84 This ḥadīth was reported by a number of companions and judged authentic (*ṣaḥīḥ*) by Aḥmad b. Ḥanbal and Ibn al-Qayyim al-Jawziyya.

85 Qur'ān, 28:77.

86 Qur'ān, 28:50.

87 Quran, 45:23.

Islam does not spread through violence

Islam requires moderation in calling people to the religion (*daʿwa*). God the Most High said, "*Call to the way of your Lord with wisdom and beautiful spiritual counsel. And reason with them in the best of manners. Surely your Lord is best aware of who has strayed from His way, and who has been guided.*"[88] The call to Islam is therefore an invitation by way of exposition, not by way of an obligatory imposition. The religion should be shown to the people without imposing it on them. Beliefs can never be rooted through compulsion, neither in the past nor in the present. God said about the people of Noah, peace be upon him: "*Shall We compel you to accept it when you are averse to it?*"[89] And God said to the Prophet: "*Will you compel mankind, against their will, to believe?*"[90] And He said, exalted is His affair: "*There is no compulsion in religion. Guidance has become clear from error.*"[91] And He also said, "*Say, 'The truth is from your Lord: let him who wills, believe, and let him who wills, deny.'*"[92]

This then is the established way of calling to Islam, whether in Mecca when the Muslims were few and weak, or whether in Medina when the Muslims were many and strong. God said to His Messenger in Medina: "*And say to those who have received the scripture and those who read not, 'Do you also submit?' If they do, they are rightly guided. But if they turn away, your duty is only to convey the message. And God sees (all) His servants.*"[93]

The history of the Prophet and his Companions is replete with examples emphasizing that Islam did not spread through conquest or at the point of the sword. The result of this is that Islam spread to the Far East and sub-Saharan African without conquest or by force of arms. Indeed, this spread occurred when the power of the Islamic State in Baghdad was weak, both militarily and politically.

---

88 Qur'ān, 16:125.

89 Qur'ān, 11:28.

90 Qur'ān, 10:99.

91 Qur'ān, 2:256.

92 Qur'ān, 18:29.

93 Qur'ān, 3:20.

It has been reported concerning 'Umar b. al-Khaṭṭāb that once an old, non-Muslim woman came to see him. He invited her to Islam, but she refused, so he left her as she was. Even then he feared that there may have been something in his words - as the Commander of the Faithful - that came across as a compulsion for her. So, he turned to his Lord in supplication, saying, "O God, I had wanted to guide her, not compel her." And he recited the verse, "*There is no compulsion in religion. Guidance has become clear from error.*"[94]

Violence breeds only hypocrisy. If violence is used in calling to Islam, then people are compelled to accept it. By this you acquire through your proselytizing only hypocrites, not believers. You gain the apparent (surrender to Islam), not the internal or hidden (belief), so there is no gain. The proper way is to call to Islam through wisdom and beautiful spiritual counsel, through dialogue and discussion.

Those who resort to violence in calling to Islam today, or who use violence to enforce their opinions on others, have completely contravened the precepts of Islamic proselytization. For these precepts we mention are the precepts of the Qur'ān.

The basic point, then, from the beginning of calling to Islam, is self-transformation. And this cannot be obtained through compulsion or violence. Usually, violence is a response to another's act of violence, or a response to the violent shackling of human liberty. So the rejection of such action becomes a violent rejection. The use of force is not permitted, however, except in cases of self-defense, or for defending (against the expropriation of) land and (the degradation of human) dignity (*'irḍ*).

God said, "*Muḥammad is the Messenger of God. And those who are with him are strong against the disbelievers but compassionate among themselves. You will see them bowing and prostrating in prayer, seeking God's grace and good pleasure.*"[95] He, the Mighty and Majestic, also said, "*If you carry out punishment, punish with the like of what you were afflicted. But if you patiently endure, verily that is a blessing for the patient.*"[96]

---

94 This narration is found in the book, *Hadhā bayān li-l-nās* (Cairo: Azhar Publishing, 1989), volume I, p. 273-294.

95 Qur'ān, 48:29

96 Qur'ān, 16:126.

And the Glorified One said, "*As for the one who attacks you, attack him as he attacked you. But fear God and know that God is with those who restrain themselves.*"[97]

Conclusion

If only the Muslims of today, in this time of controversy and strained relations, would adorn themselves with these praiseworthy characteristics. If only they internalized this glorious disposition that marked the Prophet, God's blessing and peace on him, and his companions, may God be pleased with them.

If only the Muslims would honor their guests. If only they guaranteed the safety of their neighbors from harm by their own hands and tongues. If only they fed the hungry, spread peace, and prayed while others slept. If only they removed the harm from the road. If only they encouraged each other in truth and patience. If only the youth would respect the elders, and the elders would have mercy on the youth. If only they cooperated in piety and righteousness, rather than aiding one another in sin and aggression. If only they spoke the truth to their brothers with gentle words.

If only they held fast to these fundamental roots of good character, while implementing the legal and educative principles, exemplifying in their calling to Islam purity, cleanliness, security, sincerity, justice, mercy, piety, and reliability. If only their actions were in conformity with their words, while both were in conformity with their intentions and hearts. If only they prohibited themselves from injustice, oppression, deception; from taking others' property unjustly; from transgressing into the forbidden and dishonorable things; and from disseminating abomination in any shape or form.

If the Muslims were to do all of this, we, together with the whole world, would live in peace, security, and harmony. This is the virtuous, upright way, which came with the noble Prophet. This is the way he pulled the earth to the heavens, the way he bound the hearts of the

97 Qur'ān, 2:194.

lovers to God, Glorious is He. By this the Divine connection has been extended from the highest heaven to the earth, a connection through which the horizons are ascended. By this has the unlimited attributes of God been opened, so that they may be realized by human beings in a limited way, so that people may realize a higher humanity, so that they may become worthy of the God's honor on them, and His entrusting them as His representatives on earth. By this do they become worthy of the sublime life to come: "*In an Assembly of Truth, in the Presence of the Omnipotent King.*"[98] And by this do they obtain the final goal in returning to God, for such is the sole purpose of this life. "*And that your Lord, He is the goal.*"[99]

---

98 Qur'ān, 54:55.

99 Qur'ān, 53:42.

2.

The Woman and Her Rights in Islam

Keynote address at the Islamic World International Conference Atlanta, Georgia, USA (November, 2013)

All praise to God, who created humankind from water, and from him made lineage and guardianship. He who said in His Mighty Book, *"O mankind, We created you male and female, and made you into nations and tribes that you may know one another."*[100]

Peace and blessings on (Muḥammad) the best of creation and humanity, both female and male. The one who said, "Whoever has a daughter and does not bury her alive, insult her, nor prefer his son over her, God Almighty will send him to paradise because of her." On him blessings and peace, renewed with every glance of the eye, and every audition of the ear; and the same on his family, his companions, and on all those who walk in their footsteps.

Islam considers a woman one of the pair constituting the human species. The Most High said, *"We created in pairs, male and female."*[101] A woman is thus one half of the single human soul (*nafs*). God said, *"O mankind, revere your Lord, who created you from one soul, and created its mate therefrom."*[102]

The woman is the sister (*shaqīq*) of man in origin, in upbringing, and in destiny. She shares with him the form of creation. There is no difference between them in the general aspects of religion, in the Oneness of God, in belief, in reward and punishment, and in general Divine legislation pertaining to rights and responsibilities. God said, *"Whoever works righteousness, man or woman, and has faith, verily, to him will We give a new life, a life is that is good and pure, and We will bestow on them their reward according to the best of their actions."*[103] The Prophet, peace and blessings on him, said, "Women are the sharing-partners (*shaqā'iq*) of men."[104]

The measure of honor in the presence of God is the reverence of God. God said, *"Verily the most honored of you in the sight of God is the most reverent of you."*[105] There is no more precise or eloquent expression of this meaning than the phrase, *"you are one and of the same,"* in the verse (of the Qur'ān), *"And their Lord accepted of them, and answered them,*

---

100 Qur'ān, 49:13.

101 Qur'ān, 53:45.

102 Qur'ān, 4:1.

103 Qur'ān, 16:97.

104 Ḥadīth related in collections of Abū Dāwūd and al-Tirmidhī.

105 Qur'ān, 49:13.

'Never will I disregard the work of any of you, male or female: you are one and of the same.'"[106] Men and women are thus equal in the meaning of humanity, in the generality of the religion and Divine legislation. And they are weighed equally on the scale in presence of God.

The Woman in Islam as Mother, Sister, Wife, and Daughter

Islam has honored the woman with the utmost honor and protected her with a shield of care and consideration. Islam has venerated and treasured her. It has singled her out for honor and the best treatment, whether she is a daughter, a wife, a sister, or a mother.

First of all, Islam established that both women and men were created from one source, and because of this, women and men are equal in their humanity. The Most High said, "*O humankind, fear your Lord who created you from a single person, and from it created its mate, and from them both male and female offspring.*"[107]

The state of human perfection is not the sole monopoly of men: surely women have their share in this exalted rank. The field of competition for goodness and preeminence in attaining the highest of (spiritual) degrees is open for everyone. So let women work hard and exert all efforts. Their examples in this are women like Āsiya, Maryam, Khadīja, Fāṭima, 'Ā'isha, and others in preeminence and favor, graced with emulation of the Prophets and the Righteous. The Qur'ān has provided many examples of such women, and the Muḥammadan way has given us many models of perfected women. Let us now tell the stories of some of these exemplars.

---

106 Qur'ān, 3:195.

107 Qur'ān, 4:1.

Lady Maryam, daughter of ʿImrān and mother of Jesus, upon them peace

Maryam the daughter of ʿImrān, upon her peace, was a shining image of virtue and purity. She was born an orphan, so God placed her under the care of her maternal aunt's husband, for the maternal aunt is as the mother. This husband was Zacharias (Zakariyā), upon him peace, who was a Prophet of his people.

All of this was due to God's mercy and care for Maryam. The Most High said, *"Her Lord accepted her with a beautiful acceptance. He made her grow in purity and goodness, and He entrusted her to the care of Zakariyā."*[108] As Maryam grew up, her house was the place of worship. There, she used to go into spiritual retreat. God showed her special kindness because of this, and she would be provided food from the Unseen. Whenever her aunt's husband would visit her, he would find provisions all around her. As he was the one charged with her maintenance, he would wonder where then did these things come from if he was not the one to bring them?

God the Exalted and Glorified chose Maryam and preferred her over the women of the earth. The Most High said, *"Behold! The Angels said, 'O Maryam, God has chosen you, purified you, and selected you from the women of all the world.'"*[109] Indeed, He bestowed on her the last prophet of the Children of Israel, the spirit of God and His word. The Most High said, *"And as for Maryam the daughter of ʿImrān who guarded her chastity: We breathed into her womb of Our Spirit, and she testified to the words of her Lord and His revelations. And she was one of the devotees."*[110] The Prophet Muḥammad, peace and blessing upon him, said, "Many men have obtained the rank of perfection, and among the perfected women have been Maryam the daughter of ʿImrān, Khadīja the daughter of Khuwaylid, Fāṭima the daughter of Muḥammad, and Āsiya the wife of Pharoah."

---

108 Qur'ān, 3:37.

109 Qur'ān, 3:42.

110 Qur'ān, 66:12.

Lady Yūkābid (Jochebed) the mother of Moses, upon them peace.

The Qurʾān considers the mother of Moses (Mūsā) as a model of reliance on God and submission. Her story is related in several verses of the Qurʾān. The Most High said, "*And We inspired to the mother of Moses, 'Nurse your child, and when you fear for him, put him in the river. But do not fear nor grieve. Surely We will return him to you and make him one of our Messengers.*'"[111]

The mother of Moses had a purified being, a clean heart, and a translucent spirit. She adhered to the faith of her ancestors Jacob (Yaʿqūb), Isaac (Isḥāq), and Abraham (Ibrāhīm). She had been destined to carry and give birth to a prophet from among the righteous and truthful prophets of God. Divine inspiration came to her, so her heart became tranquil and when she feared (for her son's life), she was guided to put him (on the river) in a reed basket.

Lady Āsiya, Daughter of Muzāhim, Wife of Pharaoh

Āsiya was the daughter of Muzāhim, who was the son of ʿUbayd al-Diyān, the descendant of the Pharaoh of Egypt during the time of Joseph, peace be upon him[112]. She lived in the greatest and most luxurious of palaces. Her palace was filled with maids, slaves, and servants: indeed, she lived a life of opulence and bounty. Āsiya was also the wife of the oppressive and arrogant Pharaoh of the time. He claimed to be a god, and ordered his slaves to worship him, and to sanctify no one but him, and to call him the god Pharaoh. And the refuge is with God (from such blasemphy)!

It was she who prevented Pharaoh from first killing Moses, peace be upon him, when they found him as a baby. She said to him, "He is the delight of my eye and of yours, so do not slaughter him." He said, "He may

---

111 Qurʾān, 28:7.

112 This wife of Pharoah during the time of Moses is not mentioned by Jewish and Christian scriptures, but a daughter of Pharoah who plays a similar role in the life of Moses is variously rendered as Batyah, Jehudijah, or Merrhoe.

be the delight of your eye, but not mine. As for me, I have no use for him!" Then he said, "Rather, slaughter him, for I fear this baby will make me lose my kingdom." But Āsiya interceded with him, so he left Moses for her.

When Moses, peace be upon him, began his mission proclaiming the Oneness of God, she believed in him and bore witness to the truth. In the beginning, she hid her belief out of fear from Pharaoh. But it was not long before she proclaimed her Islam and that she followed the religion of Moses, upon him peace.

This provoked the rage of Pharaoh. He killed her by tying her hands and legs to four stakes, laying her in the hot sun, and placing a boulder on her back (to slowly crush her). She endured patiently and bore the pain hoping to meet God, mighty and exalted. She called out to the Lord, Mighty and Exalted, that before her pure spirit was pulled out, that He might accept her in His presence, and that He might build for her a dwelling in Paradise. God said, *"And God set forth, as an example to those who believe, the wife of Pharaoh. She said, 'My Lord! Build me in Your presence, an abode in Paradise, and save me from Pharaoh and his doings; save me from the oppressors!'"*[113]

Lady Āmina, Daughter of Wahb, Mother of the Prophet, peace and blessings upon him

Āmina was the daughter of Wahb, the queen of all mothers, the mother of the greatest person, the most beloved of people to each of our souls, the seal of Prophets, Muḥammad, God's blessing and peace upon him. Her lineage and upbringing were of the most distinguished, due to her noted position in terms of origin, descent, nobility, and high honor. She was known as the "Flower of the Quraysh." She hailed from the honorable tribe of Zahra. She was modest, and she concealed herself from the eyes of men. Even the chroniclers of the time did not know what she looked like.

It was this mistress of exalted mothers that carried in her womb the Messenger of God, peace and blessings on him. The Prophet was only

113 Qur'ān, 66:11.

two months old when his father, ʿAbdallāh, the son of ʿAbd al-Muṭalib, died. She raised him (alone), provided for him, and looked after him, until she died in her turn, may God be pleased with her.

When she was on her deathbed, she addressed her small son Muḥammad, God's blessing and peace on him, with these lines of poetry:

May God bless you among all offspring
    O son, may you triumph in the birds' turmoil of battle
By the help of the Sovereign Lord, well acquainted (with all things)
    By my love like an early morning rain of arrows
A hundred freely grazing camels
    That He bring about what I have seen in my dream
You are the one sent to all of humanity
    You are sent to license the good, and to forbid the wrong
You are sent with the Oneness of God, and Islam
    The religion of your righteous father Abraham
So may God prevent you from worshipping idols
    And from endearing your people to these false gods.

Other Exemplary Women

There are many other women mentioned in the Qurʾān, and still others mentioned in the Prophetic narrations. They have honored positions and exalted ranks. Among them, for example, is the Lady Hājar, the mother of Ismāʿīl the Prophet, upon him peace. Her husband Abraham (Ibrāhīm) took her to (the valley of) Mecca, and he left her there without water or food or people to help her. He left her with his son Ismāʿīl as a trust. She asked him with the famous words, "Did God command you with this?" When Ibrāhīm, peace and blessing upon him, responded "Yes," she said, "Then God will not allow us to perish." Knowing that this was a Divine decree, she complied and was contented with God's judgment and wisdom. She stayed there with her son in this sanctified land (of Mecca) that people have not ceased making pilgrimage to from every deep ravine in order to worship God and seek His blessing. And God honored her by immortalizing her remembrance. An important rite of the greater and lesser pilgrimage is the *Saʿī*,[114] symbolizing Hājar's trust in God. Thus, we are always recollecting her story, and we aspire to her level of faith when she said, "Then God will not allow us to perish."

Also foremost among women is the mother of believers, the Lady Khadīja, the daughter of Khuwaylid. God created her to be the first to believe in His Prophet, and to testify to the truth of his message, may God be pleased with her. She supported him, stood by him, and sacrificed of herself and her wealth for him. She was the mother of all of his children except Ibrāhīm.

There was also ʿĀʾisha, the daughter of Abū Bakr the Truthful. She was (also) the truthful one, the daughter of the truthful one. She was a renowned jurist capable of issuing independent legal judgments. Her legal opinions were sought for many religious issues. Similarly, the scholars of Prophetic narrations recognize her for narrating the most sayings from the Prophet, God's peace and blessing on him. It was she whose honor was vindicated by the noble Qur'an, with God's words, "*Good women are for good men, and good men are for good women. They are innocent of what people impugn.*"[115]

Also foremost among women was Fāṭima, the daughter of Muḥammad, may God be pleased with her. She was known as a part of his very body. She was the mother of his two grandsons (Ḥasan and Ḥusayn), indeed the mother of all of his descendants. She is the source for all of the Prophet's household. She was the flower blossom, the devoted maiden of God, the pure, the purified. She was the best of all women. Ibn ʿAbbās related that the Prophet, God's peace and blessing upon him, said, "These four lines in the ground, do you know what they are?" We said, "God and His Messenger know best." He, peace and blessing on him, said, "The best women of Paradise are four: Khadīja daughter of Khuwaylid, Fāṭima the daughter of Muḥammad, Maryam the daughter of ʿImrān, and Āsiya the daughter of Muzāhim and wife of Pharaoh."

---

114 This rite consists of going back and forth between two small hills (Safa and Marwa) seven times, commemorating Hajar's search for water that resulted in an angel's striking the earth to produce the well of zamzam.

115 Qurʾān, 24:26.

In another *ḥadīth*, it is related that the Prophet, God's peace and blessing on him, mentioned ʿĀʾisha as also being among the best of women.

These references demonstrate that God, majestic and exalted, has greatly honored women. Indeed, all religions and messengers came with revelations that honored and protected women. If you see other than this, that is the fault of the followers of these various religions, and it is among the distortions that have crept into these religions.

The last Divine, untainted message is Islam. Islam has remained committed to these principles, as indicated by these stories, and others besides. The reality of Islam's protection and honor of women is further demonstrated by a consideration of the practices of the pre-Islamic age of ignorance. The available books of other religions, namely Christianity and Judaism, did not give any specific consideration for the rights of women. There is no particular recognition that she is a partner for man in this world. Rather, she is perceived as responsible for the so-called "original sin." Where are those who claim to advocate for women's rights in regard to these texts? How strange to ignore these texts and attack Islam, which endorsed the principle in the Qur'an, "*Never will I disregard the works of any of you, be he male or female.*"[116]

Women in the Qurʾān and Islamic Law

Islam was the first religion that honored women and gave her specific rights. It recognized her as a partner (*sharīk*) of man and gave each partner rights and obligations towards the other. Islam ensured the entirety of social, educational, and political rights between them. It gave the woman equality with the man in the essence of creation. The Qur'an clarified this in more than one verse. Concerning the equality pertaining to the essence of creation, God said, "*O humankind, fear your Lord who created you from one person, and created there from its mate, and brought forth from them both many men and women. And fear God from whom you*

116 Qurʾān, 3:195.

ask your rights and ties of relationship."[117] *"And He it was who created you from one person, then there is a place of rest and trust. Indeed, we have made plain our signs for those who understand."*[118]

God also clarified the importance of women in the marriage. She is a source of refuge, affection, and comfort. *"He it was that created you from one person and made there from its mate, so that you may dwell with her in serenity."*[119] So a woman is of great value for a man in this life. God did not obligate women to expend of their wealth for their husband or their children. Indeed, her wealth is for her alone. But if she desires, she can give charity to her husband.

There is certainly no cause for the man to object in this matter. Just as a woman is a source of serenity and comfort for a man, she has also been placed under his guardianship by his spending (on her) of his wealth and of what he has in terms of responsibility, obligations, and bodily capacity beyond her own.

Since as our Lord gave both men and women the same essential disposition to worship Him alone, and the same legal responsibilities, so He has not given preference to one gender over the other. Indeed, He made the standard of preference to be piety, righteousness, and (self) improvement. *"O humankind, We created you male and female and made you nations and tribes so that you may know one another. The most honored among you with God is the most reverent. Surely God is the Knower, Aware."*[120]

God made women equal to men in the basic Islamic legal responsibilities, in reward and punishment for what she does and what she leaves aside. *"And their Lord accepted the prayers (of both male and female), saying, 'Never will I suffer to be lost the work of any of you, whether male or female; you are of one another. So those who emigrated, and were expelled from their homes, and suffered harm in My cause, and fought and were slain, assuredly, I will remit from them their sins, and*

---

117 Qur'ān, 4:1. The reader will notice that this is the third time the Shaykh has cited this same verse, but each successive mention with more of the verse included.

118 Qur'ān, 6:9.

119 Qur'ān, 7:189.

120 Qur'ān, 49:13.

admit them into gardens beneath which rivers flow; a reward from God, and with God is the best of rewards.'"[121]

And God also said: *"Those that do evil shall be repaid the like thereof, while those that have faith and do good works, whether male or female, shall enter the Garden, where they shall be nourished beyond measure."*[122]

And He also said: *"Whoever works righteousness, man or woman, and has faith, We shall assuredly give him to a goodly life, and We will bestow upon them their reward according to the best of what they used to do."*[123]

And He said: *"And whoever does good works, whether male or female, and is a believer, such will enter the Garden, and they will not be wronged (so much as) the spot of a datestone."*[124]

And He said: *"Behold: men who surrender to God, and women who surrender, and men who believe and women who believe, and men who obey and women who obey, and men who speak the truth and women who speak the truth, and men who persevere (in righteousness) and women who persevere, and men who are humble and women who are humble, and men who give alms and women who give alms, and men who fast and women who fast, and men who guard their modesty and women who guard (their modesty), and men who remember God much and women who remember, God has prepared for them forgiveness and a great reward."*[125]

God also made men and women equal in the essential rights and obligations, for He said: *"And (women) have rights similar to those (of men) in kindness."*[126]

And He said, *"From what is left by parents and those nearest related there is a share for men and a share for women, whether the property be small or large; a legal share."*[127]

And He, glorious and exalted, made illicit the pre-Islamic Arabs' unhappiness when God provided them with girl children. He said:

---

121 Qur'ān, 3:195.

122 Qur'ān, 40:40.

123 Qur'ān, 16:97.

124 Qur'ān, 4:124.

125 Qur'ān, 33:35.

126 Qur'ān, 2:228.

127 Qur'ān, 4:7.

"When one of you receives tidings of the birth of a female his face darkens and he is filled with inward grief. With shame does he hide himself from his people because of the bad news he has had; (as if his option is) to keep the baby in contempt or bury it in the dust. How evil is their judgment."[128]

There is no shortage of noble legislative texts concerning (gender) equality in the essence of Divine commission, and in the essence of rights and responsibilities. Sometimes, the matter is unjustly reduced to the admonition of women (to remind her of her responsibilities). But, out of respect for the graciousness and modesty of her nature, we (men) must also assert her rights. So I advise men to treat women well, and to cooperate with them in goodness. As in the noble Qur'an: "*Treat them with kindness, for even if you hate them it may be that you hate a thing in which God has placed much good.*"[129] (And) "*Provide for them with fairness; the rich man according to his means and the poor man according to his. This is a binding duty upon righteous men.*"[130]

And God said (in reference to divorce), "*Lodge them in your own homes (as they require), according to your means. Do not harass them so as to make life intolerable for them. If they are with child, maintain them until they deliver their burden; and if, after that, they nurse their children, give them recompense and consult together in all reasonableness.*"[131]

And He said, "*So give to them what is owed as a duty.*"[132] And He said, "*And give them a portion of the wealth of God which He has given you.*"[133] And He said, "*So do not seek a way against them. Surely God is Most High, Mighty.*"[134] And He said, "*O you who believe, it is not lawful for you to inherit women against their will, nor to put constraint on them that you may take away a part of that which you have given them.*"[135] And He said,

128 Qur'ān, 16:58-59.

129 Qur'ān, 4:19.

130 Qur'ān, 2:236.

131 Qur'ān, 65:6.

132 Qur'ān,, 4:24.

133 Qur'ān, 24:33.

134 Qur'ān, 4:34.

135 Qur'ān, 4:19.

"(A woman must be) retained in honor or allowed to go with kindness. You may not take from them anything you have given them."[136]

It should suffice this subject that there is one chapter of the Qur'an specially named "The Women," where there is no chapter "The Men." If this is evidence of anything, it indicates the importance of women in Islam.

As for the example (*sunna*) of the Prophet, there are many narrations stressing the right of a woman, her position, the importance of honoring her, and the blessing of cohabitation with her. The noble Prophet, God's blessing and peace on him, was himself the exemplar of good character, instructing us in the manner of merciful cooperation.

According to one authentic narration taken from Ibn Māja, on the authority of Anas b. Mālik, may God be pleased with him:

> Once, the Prophet, peace be upon him, was with one of his wives, the mothers of the believers, when another wife sent a bowl of food to him. The first wife nudged the Prophet's hand while he was holding the bowl, and it fell and broke in two. The Messenger, peace be upon him, took the two parts, put them together, and collected the food. Then he said to those in the house, "Your mother became jealous, but let us eat." They ate until the bowl arrived from the house in which they were. Afterwards, the unbroken bowl was given to the Messenger, and he left the broken one is the house where it was broken.

According to the Mother of the Believers, ʿĀʾisha, may God be pleased with her, the Messenger of God, God's blessing and peace on him, said, "The best among you is the one who is kindest to his wife. And I am the kindest among you to my wives."

In *(Ṣaḥīḥ) al-Bukhārī*, Abū Hurayra, may God be pleased with him, narrated that the Messenger of God, peace be upon him said, "I commend you to the affairs of women. They were created from a delicate rib. If you bend it, it will break. If you leave it alone, it will remain bent. So make women your concern."

---

136 Qurʾān, 2:229.

Faḍḍāla b. ʿUbayd al-Anṣārī related that the Messenger of God, peace be upon him said, "Whoever believes in God and the Last Day let him be good to his neighbor and treat women kindly."

Jābir b. ʿAbdallāh Anṣārī, may God be pleased with him, narrated that the Messenger of God, peace be upon him said, "Reverence God in women. You have wedded them in God's trust. Your cohabitation with them has become lawful with God's word. Your right upon them is that they do not let into your house those whom you do not like, and if they should do so, that you may reprimand them gently. Their right upon you is that you must provide for them and clothe them in kindness."

The Messenger of God, peace be upon him said, "Women are the twin halves (*shaqāʾiq*) of men." This narration is found in all of the canonical collections, related by ʿĀʾisha, Anas b. Mālik and Um Sulaym.

Muʿāwiya al-Qusayrī related, "I went to the Messenger of God, peace be upon him, and I said, 'What do you say about our women?' He said, 'Feed them from your food and cloth them to the standard you clothe yourself; and do not hit or insult them.'"

ʿĀʾisha, may God be pleased with her, reported, "The Messenger of God, peace be upon him, never hit anything with his hand, not a woman, nor a servant, no matter how much he was struggling for the sake of God. If he was hurt from something, he never avenged himself. However, if God's prohibitions were committed, he took requital for the sake of God Almighty."

The Portrait of Honor for Women in Islam

Islam has honored women greatly. It has given her rights that were not given by any other religion or social organization. Muslim societies still observe these rights where they give women value and consideration not found in non-Muslim societies. Women in Islam have always had the right to own property, to lease, to sell and buy; and to enter into any sort of contract. A woman has the right to study and teach without contradicting anything in the religion. Some sciences are indeed obligatory for her to study, which if were neglected by either male or female, it would be deemed sinful. She has the same obligations as men except for certain matters that are unique to her in terms of rights and relevant legal rulings.

Among Islam's honor for the woman is the command for the husband to financially provide for his wife and to live with her in the best of conduct. Islam also forbids him from oppressing her and plotting evil against her. He is also prohibited from unjustly striking his wife. Islam gives her the complete right to complain of her case to her protecting relatives, or to raise her affair to a judge. Certainly, she is a human being whose honor is included in God's statement, "*We have honored the children of Adam, and provided them with transport on land and sea, and given them sustenance, both good and pure; and preferred them over most of Our creation.*"[137]

Good conduct in mutual cohabitation is not an optional command, left to the husband if he so chooses. It is an obligation. The Prophet, God's blessing and peace on him, said, "None of you may flog his wife like a slave and then sleep with her." This was related in (the ḥadīth collections of) al-Bukhārī and Muslim.

This narration is among the most rhetorically sound prohibitions against a man hitting a woman. How could a man dishonor his wife, who is just like himself, by beating her and then sleeping with her? This is not to even mention his disregard for the special cooperation and communication that should exist between them. This is not to suggest that it is legally impermissible for a man to restrain his wife, nor does it suggest that such restraint is blameworthy in every circumstance.

Another example that demonstrates Islam's honor for a woman is that it delivers her from those who denigrate her station or alienate her from her way of life. Islam has guaranteed her rights that ensure her wellbeing and elevate her status, rights requiring that the man care for her, and rights that protect her from those who might attempt to take away her dignity.

In witness to this, the Almighty said, "*And women shall have rights similar to the rights against them, according to what is equitable; but men have a degree over them.*"[138] This verse made the rights for women the same as men. In the case when the family needs a leader, then the man is worthy of

137 Qur'ān, 17:70.

138 Qur'ān, 2:228.

leadership, for his is the responsibility to financially support his family and to defend them if threatened by harm. This then is the degree mentioned when God said, "*Men are the protectors and maintainers of women.*"[139]

Part of the honor that Islam bestowed on women is that the religion permits a man to take multiple wives: two, three, or four.[140] But he may not to exceed four, and this is with the condition that he treats them fairly and equally in alimony, clothing, and residence. If the husband is unable to do so, then he is limited to one wife.

Another honor of Islam to the woman is that it assigned her a share of inheritance. A mother gets a certain share, a wife gets a certain share, a daughter and a sister and others get shares as specified in Islamic law.

It is fair that Islam assigned for a woman half the value of inheritance of a man's portion, despite the misunderstandings of some. They might say it is unfair and "how can a man get a share of two females of inheritance? Why is the share of a woman half the share of a man?" The answer is that Islam made the man financially responsible for women, while women are responsible for nurturing the family (in other ways). Also, the man pays the woman a dowry in marriage. If the woman should take the same share as the man in inheritance, it would not be fair for the male, due to his financial burden of paying the dowry, along with all other expenses. The allocation of inheritance is thus just and fair.

Overview of the Rights Islam Guarantees for Women

Some scholars of Islam have extracted a range of rights guaranteed by the justice of Islamic law toward women. Among them are the following:

Islam obligates the father to spend on the mother during her pregnancy "*And if they carry (life in their wombs), then spend (your*

139 Qur'ān, 4:34.

140 This sentence could perhaps best be explained by the response of an anonymous female licensed instructor (*muqaddima*) of the Shaykh when asked, "And how is it that polygyny may be considered among the rights that Islam grants to women?" She replied, "Although I am not personally interested in polygyny, it must be admitted that its permissibility increases the marriage options for Muslim women." Interview with translator, November 2013.

substance) on them until they deliver their burden,"[141] so as to preserve the right of her unborn child.

A prescribed penalty (*al-ḥadd*) cannot be executed on a woman if she is pregnant or breastfeeding. For instance, when the woman from tribe of Ghāmid said: "O Messenger of God, purify me from my sin (of adultery)" the Prophet replied, "not until you deliver what is in your womb". After she delivered her son, she returned and asked for the prescribed punishment of execution. He said, peace be upon him, "Go and breastfeed him until he is weaned."

Islam guarantees the mother's rights in terms of financial support and clothing: *"But he (the husband) shall bear the cost of their food and clothing on equitable terms."*[142] Furthermore, support of both mother and child is guaranteed up to the period of weaning, which extends to a few years. The father is obliged to spend on her during this period, as part of a general exigency for him to provide for his children.

Islam guarantees for women the right to inheritance regardless of her age. God says, *"If only daughters, two or more, their share is two-thirds of the inheritance; if only one, her share is half."*[143]

Islam grants the right for women to choose an appropriate husband. She also has the right to accept or reject a suitor if she is a divorcee or widow, as the Prophet, peace be upon him said, "the divorced or widowed woman cannot get married unless she is consulted." If she has never been married, her permission still needs to be sought, as the Prophet, peace be upon him said, "The virgin cannot be married without her acceptance, but silence can be a form of acceptance."

Islam has guaranteed women the right to receive a dowry: *"As you obtain happiness from them, give them their dowries (at least) as prescribed."*[144]

141 Qur'ān, 65:6.

142 Qur'ān, 2:233.

143 Qur'ān, 4:11.

144 Qur'ān, 4:24.

Islam grants women the right to divorce herself from her husband (*khulʿ*), according to the words of the Prophet, God's blessing and peace on him, "Take back the garden and divorce her."[145]

Islam gave rights for divorced women: "*For divorced women maintenance (should be provided) on a reasonable (scale). This is a duty on the righteous.*"[146]

Islam gives the widow a share of her husband's inheritance. God Almighty says, "*Their share is a quarter from what you have left them, if you leave no child; but if you leave a child, they receive an eighth.*"[147]

Islam omitted the waiting period after divorce (ʿidda) in the case when a divorce occurs prior to consummation. God the Almighty says, "*O you who believe! When you marry believing women, and then divorce them before you have touched them, no period of waiting have you to count in respect of them.*"[148]

Islam ensures the rights of an orphan girl and gives her a share of the spoils of war. God says, "*And know that out of all the booty that you may have acquired (in war), a fifth share is assigned to God and to the Messenger, and to near relatives and orphans.*"[149] Islam also gave the orphan girl a share from the state treasury. God Almighty says, "*What God has bestowed on His Messenger (and taken away) from the people of the townships, belongs to God, to His Messenger and to kindred and orphans.*"[150] Islam also granted her a share out of the division of wealth, "*And at the time of the division of inheritance, give to the relatives,*

---

145 Thābit b. Qays had given his wife a garden for a wedding dowry, but after their marriage, the wife (Ḥabība bint Sahl) came to the Prophet complaining, "I do not blame Thābit for any defects in his character or his religion, but I cannot endure to live with him." In parallel narrations Ḥabība's dislike was on account of a lack of attraction, with her adding, "Were it not for the fear of God, I would spit in his face when he entered my presence." So the Prophet ordered Thābit to take back his garden and divorce her. Various versions of this narration are found in the *ḥadīth* collections of Abū Dāwūd, al-Bukhārī, Ibn Māja, and al-Nasāʾī. See https://sunnah.com/search?q=Habibah+Thabit+ibn+Qays (Accessed by translator, 2 July 2022). Divorce initiated by women by returning the dowry is called *khulʿ* in Islamic law.

146 Qur'ān, 2:241.

147 Qur'ān, 4:12.

148 Qur'ān, 33:49.

149 Qur'ān, 8:41.

150 Qur'ān, 59:7.

or orphans."[151] It also gave her a share from charity, "*Say, Whatever you spend of good must be for parents and kindred and orphans."*[152]

Islam defended the rights of women in her social life and maintained her safety and good relations with relatives. God has forbidden a man to combine in marriage a woman with her sister or aunt, as referred to in the Quran and in the Ḥadīth.

Islam defended the dignity of women by making any accusation of fornication without evidence punishable by flogging; "*And those who launch a charge against chaste women, and produce not four witnesses (to support their allegations), flog them with eighty stripes."*[153]

Islam honored the woman as a mother, and obligated good treatment towards her, and warned against saying words of contempt to her. Islam imposed financial support for wet-nurses; a right shared between the wet-nurse and the baby: "*And if they nurse your (offspring), give them their recompense."*[154] Islam ensured a woman's right to a home: "*Let the women live in the same style as you live, and according to your means."*[155] Islam has excused women from certain obligations for the sake of their wellbeing, for they were exempt from fasting if breastfeeding or pregnant.

We ask God, the Almighty to guide us to righteousness in this religion. He is the Patron of righteousness and all capacity is with Him. May God's peace be upon you, along with His mercy and blessing.

---

151 Qur'ān, 4:8.

152 Qur'ān, 2:215.

153 Qur'ān, 24:4.

154 Qur'ān, 65:6.

155 Qur'ān, 65:6.

3.

Fraternity in God

Versions of Addresses given at the Islamic World International Conference, Atlanta, Georgia USA (January 2011 and November 2013), and Luton, United Kingdom (August 2014)

Praise to God, who engendered fraternity between souls, who brought them together in intimacy before the appearance of forms. He said in the distinguished revelation (of the Qur'ān), "*The believers are brothers, so make peace between your brothers. And fear God, so that you may have mercy.*"[156] And blessing and peace on the master of existence, the spiritual assistance of existence, our master Muḥammad. The Prophet Muḥammad, blessings and peace be upon him, is grace bestowed, mercy conferred, and the torch of guidance brightly lit. He said, "I have been sent as a mercy and not for chastisement." And God Most High said about His Prophet, *"And indeed you are of tremendous character."*[157]

The Prophet was he who engendered bonds of brotherhood between those who left Mecca for Medina (*al-muhājirūn*) and the inhabitants of Medina who helped them (*al-anṣār*). His aspiration was to unite people upon the sanctity of brotherhood, love, and trust, so that they may become beautiful exemplars for all of humanity, with no regard to skin color or language. He said, "The Muslim is the brother to the Muslim. He does not harm him. He does not forsake him. He does not disdain him." And he said, "The believer loves for his brother what he loves for himself." May God's blessing and peace be upon the Prophet, on his family and his companions, and on all those who are guided by him to the Day of Judgment.

The subject of our talk today is fraternity in God, or fraternity in Islam, and these two mean the same thing.

God conferred a great blessing on all Muslims when he made of us brothers in God. Brotherhood in God the Most High has tremendous fruits and wondrous benefits, of which the Muslim avails himself in this world and the afterlife. Among these benefits is that the love of God, the majestic and exalted, is due to the one who implements the precepts of brotherhood. This is apparent in the story related by Imam Muslim, concerning the man who visited his brother in God, so God sent to him

---

156 Qur'ān, 49:10.

157 Qur'ān, 68:4.

an Angel, who informed him of God's love for him (on account of his love for his brother).[158]

Another benefit of brotherhood is the perfection of faith and the taste of its sweetness. In the two authenticated *ḥadīth* collections (of Bukhari and Muslim), there is the report of Anas, may God be pleased with him, concerning three types of people who will taste the sweetness of faith. Among them is the man who loves his brother for no other reason except for the sake of God.[159] Also (found) in the *ḥadīth* collection of Abū Dāwūd (is the following narration): "Who loves for the sake of God, and hates for the sake of God; who gives for God's sake and holds back for God's sake: this one has perfected his faith."

A third benefit of fraternity for God's sake is obtaining refuge in the protective shade that issues from the very shade of God's Throne on the Day of Resurrection. It has been related in the two most rigorously authenticated *ḥadīth* compilations that Abū Hurayra, God be pleased with him, narrated that the Prophet, blessings and peace be upon him, said, "God will grant shade to seven people on a Day in which there will be no shade except His shade." And among them are two men who love one another for the sake of God: they meet one another in this state and depart in this state.

A fourth benefit is that fraternity ensures unity in Islam and harmony within the Muslim community, and this is what brings together the strength and power of the community. For the Prophet, blessings and peace be upon him, said, "A believer with regard to another believer is like a building, one part supports the other."

A final benefit of fraternity is that love and the forging the bonds of brotherhood for the sake of God are causes for admission into the

---

158 The full ḥadīth in *Ṣaḥīḥ Muslim* is as follows: Abu Hurayra reported that the Prophet said, "A man set out to visit a brother (in faith) in another town and God sent an angel on his way. When the man met the angel, the latter asked him, 'Where do you intend to go?' He replied, 'I intend to visit my brother in this town.' The angel asked, 'Do you have anything to gain from him?' He said, 'No, I have no desire except to visit him because I love him for the sake of God, the exalted and glorious.' Then the angel said, 'I am messenger to you from God (to inform you) that God loves you as you love him.'"

159 The full *ḥadīth* of the Prophet Muḥammad, as related by Anas, is as follows: "Whoever possesses the following three qualities will taste the sweetness of faith: the one to whom God and His Messenger have become dearer than anything else; the one who loves a person and he loves him only for God's sake; and the one who hates to revert to disbelief after God has save him from it just as he would hate to be thrown into a fire."

Garden of Paradise. As the Messenger of God, blessings and peace be upon him, said, "You will not enter the Garden until you believe, and you will not believe until you love one another." And this is well known. The noble Quran and Prophetic traditions are replete with similar counsel. Whoever takes firm hold of this advice finds success, and whoever seeks the way to God with this arrives.

The greatest Messenger, blessings and peace upon him, said in a *ḥadīth* related in *Ṣaḥīḥ Muslim* on the authority of Abū Hurayra, may God be pleased with him: "Do not envy one another. Do not hate one another. Do not turn your back on one another. Do not undercut one another in business transactions. Be brothers in worshipful servitude of God. The brother is the brother to the Muslim. He does not wrong him. He does not forsake him. He does not disdain him. Piety is here! Piety is here!" and he pointed to his heart. "All of a Muslim is inviolable to another Muslim: his blood, his wealth, and his honor. It is enough evil that man should look down on his Muslim brother."

Also found in the *ḥadīth* collections of Ibn Ḥazīma and Ibn Ḥabān is the statement of ʿAbdallāh b. ʿUmar b. al-Khaṭṭāb, may God be pleased with them both: "The Messenger of God, may God's blessing and peace be upon him, addressed the people on the day of Mecca's conquest (*yawm al-fatḥ*), and said, 'O people! Surely God has driven from you the pride and boasting of the age of pagan ignorance. O people! Mankind is of two types: the first is a pious believer, honored in the presence of God; the second is a wretched corrupted person, humiliated in the presence of God. *O Mankind, we have created you from a (single) male and female and made of you nations and tribes so that you may come to know one another. Indeed, the most honored of you in the presence of God is the most pious.*"[160]

In the Musnad of Aḥmad (b. Ḥanbal) it is related from Abū Naḍra, may God be pleased with him, that the Prophet, may God bless him and grant him peace, said in his (farewell) sermon [...], "O people, surely your Lord is One, and your father is one. There is no preference for the Arab over the foreigner, nor for the black over the red, except through piety. The best of you in the presence of God is the most pious."

---

160 Qur'ān, 49:13.

These verses and *ḥadīth* clarify for us the importance of the Islamic brotherhood, and the importance of love for the sake of God, the magnificent and exalted. The brotherhood of faith opens for each Muslim a great door anywhere in the world. And what is more beautiful than to feel, as the Muslim feels, that he has a brother or sister in every land he should visit. In any place and from every nation, he has the same rights as his brother, and also has the same duties, if only the guidelines left for us by the greatest Messenger, God's peace and blessings upon him, were put into practice.

The brotherhood of faith is a brotherhood above that of tribalism or nationalism. There is nothing that restrains truthful brotherhood, brothers bound together for the sake of God, majestic and exalted. And God is above all restrictions. Let everyone be as one body, in which abides one spirit, directed by one intellect, having one goal. The Messenger, God's peace and blessing upon him, said, "The semblance of the believers in their mutual love, mercy, and sympathy is like one body. If one part of it complains, all of the body parts call on each other to help it, awake in the night and hot with fever." This type of brotherhood is above the brotherhood of family, above the brotherhood of tribe, above the brotherhood of the nation. This is why the Arabs say, "There is many a brother (for you) to whom your mother did not give birth."

Islam enjoins on the followers of this true religion mutual cooperation and solidarity in order to attain what has been ordained in it of exalted aspirations: serving their interests in this life and fulfilling their hopes of reward in the next. Similarly, Islam prohibits its followers to assist each other in destroying the interests of others, whether they are individuals or communities, even if it is in the interests of the Muslims to do so. This would be considered sin and transgression. The Most High has said, "*Assist one another in righteousness and devotion, do not assist one another in sin and aggression.*"[161]

In this time more than ever, we need to apply this Divine principle. We are living in a time when materialism has exceeded its proper bounds,

161 Qur'ān, 5:2.

coming to predominate over everything. The result is selfishness and greed, the love of this world, the public circulation of evil among people, and the scarcity of goodness and those who guide to it. If humanity has reached such a state, then they have arrived to the state of "loss", mentioned in God's statement, *"By the (token of) Time (through the ages), surely mankind is in a state of loss, except those who believe and do good works, and exhort one another to truth and patience."*[162] In these verses, the Lord of Might and Majesty swears by Time, that the life of the children of Adam is in loss if they do not believe or do good works, and that the life of the believers and righteous doers is also in loss, except if they assist one another in exhorting to the good.

The concept of mutual assistance or cooperation in the true religion means the understanding of (different) opinions, unity of the goal and the congregation of hearts for its attainment. It is the bringing forth of every aspect of enjoined goodness for accomplishing this cooperation; and it is refraining from every aspect of evil that we have been commanded to forsake. And surely the servant is first commanded to perform this himself, then to help others of his Muslim brothers with the same. In the congregation is strength and in differentiation is weakness, and the weak are scattered. As the poet has said,

> If put together, arrows cannot be broken
> But if separated, they are broken one by one.

God the Glorious commissioned us with assisting one another in righteousness (*birr*), and He joined righteousness with reverence (*taqwa*). The pleasure of God the Most High is found in reverence to Him, and the contentment of people is found in righteousness. Who combines the pleasure of God with the contentment of the people has his happiness fulfilled and his blessing extended everywhere.

Righteousness (*birr*) is a comprehensive term for all that God loves and all that pleases Him. This could be good works performed publicly or secretly, either fulfilling the rights of God, or fulfilling the rights of human

---

162 Qur'ān, 103:1-3.

beings. Reverence (*taqwa*) here indicates a comprehensive term for abandoning all that God and His messenger dislike, both publicly and secretly.

In explaining the Qur'ān verse, "*And assist one another in righteousness and reverence*," al-Qurṭubī[163] said: "This means to help one another, urging one another to fulfill the command of God the Most High and to cut oneself off from what He has prohibited, abstaining from it completely."

As for God's saying, "*And do not assist one another in sin and aggression*:" the meaning of "sin" here is whatever causes a person to disobey God; and the meaning of "aggression" (*'idwān*) here is transgression against the creation, whether against their blood, their property, or their honor. For every disobedience and oppression, the servant of God must first prevent himself from it, then assist others in abandoning it. The practical proof of Islam's disavowal and repudiation of aggression is found in His saying, "*And do not assist one another in sin and aggression*." Thus has God prohibited mutual assistance in evil and aggression, and even completely forbidden aggression in all its forms. The Most High said, "*But do not engage in aggressive, brutal action, for God does not love the transgressors.*"[164]

Fraternity on the basis of the Prophetic model

The Prophet, God's blessing and peace on him, laid the foundation for the edifice of good deeds in Islam. In the first hour of the first day of his arrival in Medina the Radiant, he instructed the Companions, may God be pleased with them, to build the mosque. They rallied their forces to help the effort, and began construction of the mosque, for it would be the first foundation in the call to Islam. The Prophet himself participated in this construction, as a powerful incentive for work and sincere sacrifice, and as a means of showing them that Islam is a religion of work, effort, and

163 Imam Abū 'Abdallāh al-Qurṭubī (d. 1273) was a renowned Islamic scholar from Cordoba, Spain. His *Tafsīr al-Qurṭubī*, comprising twenty volumes, is one of the most famous works of Qur'ān exegesis in Sunni Islam.

164 Qur'ān, 2:190. Yusuf Ali translates the full verse as follows: "Fight in the cause of God those who fight you, but do not transgress limits; for God loveth not transgressors."

mutual assistance. He also demonstrated that the Muslim leader must be humble, and not be too full of pride to work with his people or to fight with his soldiers. When the Companions, my God be pleased with them, saw their Prophet working alongside them with his two blessed hands, they dedicated themselves completely to the work.

The same thing happened during the digging of the trench (*khandaq*),[165] which was a long and great trench requiring large effort to dig. If it had not been for the participation of the Prophet, the Companions could not have finished digging the trench before the attack of the forces allied against them (*aḥzāb*).

The Prophet, God's blessing and peace on him, also demonstrated the importance and great influence of mutual assistance in the survival of societies. He engendered brotherhood between the "Emigrants" from Mecca (*Muhājirīn*) and the "Helpers" in Medina (*Anṣār*), so that they assisted one another in righteousness and devotion (*taqwā*). Their fraternity provided a most admirable example of love, sincerity, and altruism; and of the love for the good of one's brothers. History had never before witnessed the like. This was because the way that love was shared between the hearts of the Emigrants and the Helpers, the way that they assisted each other and preferred their brothers over themselves, was absolutely not for worldly interest. It was a love for the sake of God, for the sake of His pleasure.

There are several Prophetic narrations urging mutual assistance in righteousness and devotion. Al-Bukhārī and Muslim relate on the authority of Anas, may God be pleased with him, that the Prophet said: "None of you believes until he loves for his brother what he loves for himself." And Muslim relates on the authority of Abū Hurayra, may God be pleased with him, that the Prophet said, "God is in the assistance of the servant so long as the servant is in the assistance of his brother." And he said, "Who is able to help his brother should help him." Al-Nasāʾī and al-Ḥākim relate that (ʿAbdallāh) Ibn Abī Awfā reported that the Messenger was neither

165 This was built to ward off an invading army of some 10,000 sent from Mecca to exterminate the nascent Muslim community. The "Battle of the Trench," as the ensuing engagement came to be called, took place in 627 C.E. or 5 A.H. The trench was effective in rendering the attackers' cavalry useless, helping to produce a stalemate on the battlefield.

disdainful nor too proud to walk with the widow, the poor person, or the slave, for the time it took him to provide them what they needed.

The Prophet, God's blessing and peace on him, also said, "The one who guides to good is the same as the one who does the good." And he said: "The relationship of the Muslim to his fellow Muslim is as one building, each part of it strengthening the other." Commenting on this narration, al-Qurṭubī said, "This similitude is meant to encourage believers to assist and help one another, (emphasizing) that this is a matter of great importance which must be implemented, just as a building cannot be completed or be of use until each part holds firmly to another part, thereby strengthening it. If this were not the case, each part would become loosened, and the building would collapse. The same is true for the believer: he cannot succeed in this world or in his religion except by mutual assistance and support. Without this, he is incapable of undertaking any exigency or defending himself against any harm. At such a point, the very structure of his worldly affairs and his religion are incomplete, and he follows the way of those who met with destruction before him."

Love and brotherhood are essential for the perpetuation of mutual assistance between Muslims. The human soul does not attain intimacy except with the one she loves. "The spirits of men are like recruited soldiers. Those that have known each other become connected and those that have not known each other part ways."[166] This was the reason the Prophet encouraged his community to get to know each other, to visit each other. He established rights owed to every Muslim, and if they were to be implemented and guarded, affection would enter the hearts of the Muslims. Such rights include visiting the sick person, asking for mercy on the one who sneezes, the greeting of peace to those you know and those you do not know, and sharing in each other's happiness and sadness. All of this is a solid foundation for the maintenance and continuation of affection between the Muslims, and an immediate cause of their mutual assistance.

Intelligent folk concur on the excellence of good character, gentleness, and good companionship. Islam has devoted considerable attention

---

166 *Ḥadīth* on the authority of Abū Hurayra reported in *Ṣaḥīḥ Muslim*.

to this matter, and the legal texts are replete with guidance, praise, and encouragement towards good character. Indeed, the Messenger, God's blessing and peace on him, went the furthest in this when he said, "I have only been sent to perfect the noble traits of good character." And in these words of his there is much for contemplation. He also said: "My Lord refined my manners with the best of moral refinement."

Since he was sent to perfect the noble traits of good character, and since it was his Lord who refined his manners, we find him the best of mankind in manners, the most perfect of character, the most beautiful in keeping companionship. The Glorious Lord described him thus: "*And indeed you have a tremendous character*."[167] There is no good character trait except that the Messenger had acquired the most bountiful allotment of it. His Companions described the excellence of his character in numerous narrations. For example, ʿAlī b. Abī Ṭālib, may God be pleased with him, said: "The Messenger of God, God's blessing and peace on him, had the widest heart among mankind. He was the most truthful in speaking among mankind. He was the gentlest of them in nature, and the most noble in companionship." This narration is found in collection of al-Tirmidhī.

God the Exalted likewise described him as being gentle with his Companions, for He said, "*So it was by the mercy of God that you were gentle with them*."[168] His excellent character was clearly manifest in his relations with his Companions, for he used to answer the invitation of any who invited him, and he used to accept the gift offered to him and then similarly requite the giver. He used to unite them, and not cause them to disperse. He used to inquire after them and visit them. He used to give everyone who sat with him the attention he required, to the point his sitting companion would think there was no one so honored in the gathering as himself. And he would not confront anyone of them with something he did not like.

Al-Tirmidhī and Abū Dāwūd relate that Anas, may God be pleased with him, said: "I served the Messenger of God for ten years, and he never once uttered a word of disapproval to me. And he never asked me why

167 Qur'ān, 68:4.

168 Qur'ān, 3:159.

I did something I did, or why I did not do something I did not do." 'Abdallāh b. Jarīr al-Bajalī, as reported in Ibn Māja, similarly remembered the way the Prophet dealt with him. He said: "Since I embraced Islam, the Messenger of God never prevented me from seeing him, and every time I saw him, he would meet me with a smile. Once I complained to him that I had trouble stabilizing myself on horseback. Then he touched me on the chest with his hand and said, 'O God, make him firm, guide him and make him a source of guidance.'"

These are but a few examples of the excellence of his character and companionship, a drop from a flood, the whole of which could not be contained in articles or books. We ask God to provide us with good character and good deeds.

The Prophet encouraged Muslims to mold themselves with good character traits in all situations. Thus 'Abdallāh b. 'Amrū b. al-'Āṣ, may God be pleased with them, related that the Prophet said, "The most beloved among you to me are those with best character." This has been reported in *(Ṣaḥīḥ) al-Bukhārī.*

A man once said to the Prophet: "O Messenger of God, I have relatives with whom I try to join relations, but they cut me off. I treat them well, but they mistreat me. I am forbearing toward them, but they ignore me." The Prophet said, "If you are as you say, then you are sinking them in hot ashes, and God will be your assistance over them so long as you continue in this manner." This has been reported in *(Ṣaḥīḥ) Muslim.*

The Prophet said, "I am the guarantor of a house in the heights of Paradise built for the one who beautifies his character." And he said, "The most beloved of you to me, and the one who will sit closest to me on the Day of Judgment, is one with the best character." And He said, "There is nothing heavier than good character in the weighing of a believer on the Day of Judgment, for surely God hates the abominable and the obscene." And in another narration: "The one who possesses good character will attain a rank above the one who has (only) fasted and prayed."

The Prophet said: "The most complete in his faith is one with the best character, and the best of you is one the who is best to his family." And in another narration, the wording is "...the best of you is the one who is best to women."

It has also been narrated from him: "The most beloved to God of His servants are the best of them in character." And it has been reported that he said, "Verily these traits of good character are from God the Most High, so for whomever God desires good, He provides him with good character." And he reportedly said, "Surely good character melts away mistakes like water melts ice."

The Requirements of Brotherhood

There is much textual evidence stressing the merits and requirements of brotherhood and mutual love for the sake of God the magnificent and exalted. Indeed, a great reward, as previously mentioned, has been promised in this world and the next for brotherhood in God, for meeting together in Him and because of Him, and for mutual love in Him.

Brotherhood in God is only from the blessing of God and His grace. The Lord, glorious and exalted is He, says, "*Remember the blessing of God on you when you were enemies and He brought your hearts together, and you became, by His blessing, brothers.*"[169] Thus has God mighty and majestic made brotherhood a divine provision.

Brotherhood entails offering advice and mutual encouragement in patience. The Most High said, "*By the testimony of time through the ages, surely mankind is in loss. Except those who believe and work righteous deeds, who encourage each other in truth, and encourage each other in patience.*"[170]

Brotherhood requires patience with the brothers and bearing with the harm that may come from them. The Most High said, "*As for the one who is patient and forgives, surely that is true constancy.*"[171]

Brotherhood includes guarding secrets and covering over the private matters of the believers. Such was related by Muslim on the authority of Abu Hurayra: "Whoever covers over (the faults of) a Muslim, God will cover (his faults) on the Day of Judgment.

---

169 Qur'ān, 3:103.

170 Qur'ān, 103:1-3.

171 Qur'ān, 42:43.

Brotherhood means cooperating in righteousness and piety. The Muslim is small by himself but many with his brothers. The Most High said, "*Cooperate in righteousness and piety, do not assist one another in sin and enmity.*"[172]

Brotherhood offers solace and support for the Muslim brother when calamity descends on him. In such states, the truthful brother appears out of love for his Muslim brother. That is why one wise poet said, "When demands become distressing, they are lessened by one who helps."

Brotherhood involves dealing with the brothers, and the beautification of (one's own) character. The Prophet, God's blessing and peace on him, said, "Righteousness is the beautification of character." God our Lord established (the incumbency of) brotherhood with His words, "*Indeed, the believers are a brotherhood.*"[173]

Many *ḥadīth* substantiate this understanding that the brotherhood of Islam develops from the love and oneness of God the Most High. Indeed, the love of the believers and loyalty to them necessitates the love of God and loyalty to Him. Whoever loves God and is loyal to Him, surely he must love for the sake of God, Glorious and Exalted is He. God says, "*Believing men and believing women, they are protectors of each other.*"[174] The Prophet, God's blessing and peace on him, said, "You will not enter Paradise until you have faith. And you will not have faith until you love one another." This has been related in *Ṣaḥīh Muslim*.

Indeed, the Prophetic *ḥadīth* are replete with (exhortations of) similar lofty sensibilities. All of this points to the importance of brotherhood in God, and brotherhood in the religion. God thus exhorts us in the Qur'an, "*Surely the believers are a brotherhood, so correct the affairs between your brothers.*"[175] And He said in another verse, "*Call them by (the names) of their fathers, that if more equitable in the sight of God. And if you do not know their fathers, they (they are) your brethren in the religion.*"[176] And in *ḥadīth*, the Messenger, God's blessings and peace on him, said,

172 Qur'ān, 5:2.

173 Qur'ān, 49:10.

174 Qur'ān, 9:71.

175 Qur'ān, 49:10.

176 Qur'ān, 33:5.

"I am the intercessor for any two men who become brothers for the sake of God, from the time of my being sent until the Final Hour."

Brotherhood in God, magnificent and exalted is He, is the solid foundation for the revival of the spirit of love in God. Love in God is a distinguishing feature (*khaṣla*), the possessor of which is envied on the Day of Judgment. It has been narrated by Muʿādh b. Jabal, may God be pleased with him, that the Messenger of God, peace and blessings upon him, said, "God, Mighty and Majestic, says, 'Those who love each other for the sake of My Majesty, for them are pulpits of light, envied by the Prophets and martyrs on the Day of Judgment, on account of their proximity to the Real, magnificent and exalted is He.'"

The Prophet's formation of brotherhood bore fruit among his companions in Medina. And subsequently, (this brotherhood) has brought together and benefitted peoples and tribes of diverse ethnicities and languages. They have become brothers by the Prophet's blessing, both in his lifetime and in that of the righteously guided successors after him. And now, all of us Muslims must return to this covenant in order to be strengthened with the completion of faith. Surely this (Muslim) community will not have its affairs corrected except by that which corrected the affairs of those before us. And this was related by the Prophet himself, upon him blessing and peace.

I offer sincere counsel to Muslims wherever they are: forge the bonds of brotherhood for the sake of God and in the way of submission (*al-Islām*). Let us come to a common understanding: treat well all of creation, especially humanity, and conduct ourselves properly with everyone. This applies even to those who are outside of this sublime religion [of Islam]. God, the Blessed and the Exalted, said, "*God does not forbid you [to be benevolent] with those who have not waged war against you on account of [your] religion and who have not driven you from your homes. God loves those who act with justice.*"[177]

It was related that the Messenger of God, blessings and peace be upon him, said, "Whoever treats well all of creation but abuses a cat, he is not a righteous person." So let us beautify our characters and rectify our dealings with everything in order to obtain the pleasure and love of

177 Qurʾān, 60:8.

God, glorious and exalted. The Prophet, peace and blessings on him, said, "All creation is the family of God, the most beloved of them to God are those that benefit His family."

Conclusion

The best way to conclude this lecture is with the narration from Hind b. Abī Hālah, the stepson of the Prophet, God's blessing and peace on him, and the son of the lady Khadīja, may God be pleased with her. He described the Messenger of God by saying:

> The Messenger of God, God's blessing and peace on him, was in a state of constant sadness and persistent contemplation. He had no rest. He did not speak except out of necessity, and he was prone to long periods of silence. He began and ended his words with his entire mouth, not from the corners of his lips. He spoke in a complete manner, phrase by phrase without surplus or truncation. He was mild-tempered, neither harsh nor weak. He esteemed every blessing, no matter how small, and never caste blame on anything. He did not find blame in different tastes in food, nor did he praise them. When standing up for the truth of something, his anger did not subside until the truth was made victorious, but he did not get angry nor take revenge for his own sake. He was magnanimous and forbearing. When he pointed to something, he did so with his whole hand. If he was surprised by something, he turned over his palms. When he was angry, he turned his face away, and if he was happy, he lowered his eyes. Most of his laughter manifested in smiling, but when he laughed his teeth shone white like hail stones.
>
> He guarded his tongue except from what concerned him. He brought his companions together and did not divide them. He honored the noble person of every tribe and appointed him a leader over them. He cautioned people and was on guard among them without depriving any one of glad tidings. He inquired after his companions, and he asked people about people. He enjoined good and enacted it, and he

renounced the bad and avoided it. He was moderate, not complicated. Nothing escaped his attention, lest others become negligent or distracted. He was prepared for every situation. He was never found wanting in what was right, nor did he exceed the limits.

He was surrounded with good people. The most preferred of them to him were those who spread good advice, and the greatest of them in station to him were the best of them in providing solace and support to others.

He never sat down nor stood up without remembering God. He did not lay claim to particular places, meaning he did specify for himself a place. If he came upon a gathering, he sat in the nearest place available, and urged others to do the same. He gave everyone sitting with him his proper due, so that each one thought there was no one present more honored than himself. If someone came to him for something, he would stay with him until the other departed. Whoever asked him for something would either receive it or receive kind words.

He was generous with people through his grace and good character, so he became a father to them, and they all had equal rights to him. The most preferred of them to him was the most pious. His gathering was one of gentleness, modesty, patience, and trust. People did not raise their voices too loud, nor were inviolable things transgressed upon. People did not fear harm, and they had mutual affection through pious devotion. They treated the elderly with respect and the youth with mercy. They helped those in need, and they welcomed strangers.

He was always cheerful, and he had an easy disposition and gentle character. He was not harsh or course, neither did he speak loudly or obscenely. He did not scorn people, nor did he flatter them. He overlooked what displeased him and left it. He abandoned three things in respect to himself: hypocrisy, hoarding, and that which did not concern him. He abandoned three things in respect to other people: he did not censure anyone, he did not scold them, nor did he try to find out their secrets. He spoke only when there was benefit in speaking. When he spoke, the people sitting with him were as still as if there were birds on their heads. When he was silent, they talked, but did not quarrel in his presence. When someone talked in front of him,

> they kept quiet until he had finished. Their conversation was about the first topic raised.
> He laughed at what amused them, and he was surprised at what surprised them. He was patient with a stranger who had course language. He said, 'When you find someone asking for something he needs, then give it to him.' He did not look for praise except to counterbalance something. He did not interrupt anyone speaking until that person had himself come to an end of speaking or had stood up.

The narrator was then asked about the silence of God's Messenger, so he said:

> His remaining silent was for four reasons: forbearance, caution, appraisal, and reflection. His appraisal was for constantly observing and listening to the people. His reflection was upon what would endure and what would vanish. His forbearance was found in patience. Nothing provocative angered him. His caution was on account of four things: adopting something good that would become an example for others; abandoning something bad that others would abandon; striving to determine what was beneficial to his community; and establishing for them what would combine the blessing of this world with that of the next.

This narration from Hind b. Abī Hālah, the stepson of the Prophet and son of Sayyida Khadīja may God be pleased with her, is found in al-Bayhaqī's *Dalā'il al-nubuwwa*, where the author provides plentiful evidence of its reliability.

> We ask God the glorious and exalted to beautify our characters, and to make us among those who mutually assist one another in righteousness and devotion, and keep us away from sin and aggression, and from assisting each other in that.
> O God, guide the Muslim youth, men and women. Guide the rulers over the Muslims to what is good for the Muslim community. O God, bless the organizers of this conference, and those who helped and

supported them, and everyone who participated, whether a large amount or small.

O God, grant blessings and peace on Muḥammad, the one who opened, the one who sealed, and on his family, and may this prayer be equal to his worth, and surely his worth is exceedingly great. *"Glory be to your Lord, the Lord of Might, free is He from what they describe. And peace on the Messengers. And all praise is due to God, Lord of all the worlds."*[178]

---

178 Qur'ān, 37:180-182.

4.

The Stars of Guidance Concerning the Position of the Prophet Muhammad, God's peace and blessings on him

Speeches Delivered for the Celebration of the Mawlid
Luton, UK (2012) and Kumasi, Ghana (2014)

In the name of God, the Compassionate, the Merciful. All praise to God, who sent His Messenger with the guidance and the religion of truth to proclaim it over all religions, even if the disbelievers and polytheists may detest it.

And may the peace and blessings of God be upon our Master Muḥammad, the praised one, the source of tranquility and hope, and the splendor of the heavens and earth, whose blessings brought an end to oppression, spiritual blindness, and grief. He is the best who led the ranks of the chosen messengers. He implemented the divine commands. Through his blessings, the (disbelieving) Jinn were prevented from the Garden of Eden. He provided warning against the delusions of doubt and sin. He is the culmination of glory, and he obtained a unique distinction with God. He holds the banner of praise, and he possesses the station of praise.

O God, send blessings and peace upon him to the extent of Your knowledge, O Hearer of prayers. Let this be a continual blessing, lasting for as long as Your dominion, O You who will never perish. And upon his family, those pleasant beings, may blessings be showered continuously.

O God, be pleased with his companions, by whose blessings all harm has left us. And may He be pleased with the followers of the companions, those who keep the communal Friday prayer and who join in congregation with the (Muslim) community, the people of the noble Prophetic example (*sunna*). And may You be pleased with those of Your friendship (*wilāya*) and its Seal, and with the people of the spiritual flood (*fayḍa*) and its Imam.

It is from the major signs of the last days that we gather in this place in order to discuss with our Muslim brethren about the great rank of our prophet, may the blessings and peace of God be upon him; that we (must) gather to prove that he is indeed the best of creation and the best of humanity. Verily, this is what our faith (*īmān*) is based on, without which faith cannot be affirmed, for the key to Islam cannot be attained except through him. It is clear that one's testimony of faith is not sound if one only proclaims the oneness of God, unless the testimony is coupled with testifying that Muḥammad is the Messenger of God. It is only then that one has affirmed his Islam. This proclamation is consequently pronounced in the call (*ādhān*) to every prayer, in the standing up (*iqāma*) for every prayer, at the moment of death, and in the grave at the time of questioning. This formula is also written throughout paradise, and it was written on God's throne prior to the creation of the heavens, earth, the Tablet and the Pen.

How is it possible that God could have joined His name to that of Muḥammad without significance? How is it possible that there could be someone better than Muḥammad, who was not mentioned in this way?

Our Master Muḥammad, peace and blessings be upon him, is preferred over all the Prophets and Messengers, the Angels brought near (to the Divine Presence), all the righteous servants of God, and the entire creation, whether they are measured individually or all together. If all their merits were combined on one side of a scale and his merit, peace and blessing be upon him, on another, his merit would outweigh theirs.

This reality is self-evident for our understanding as Muslims. We are only here to defend this reality as those who have been entrusted with the defense of the Messenger of good character against the biased aspersions recently directed at him, peace be upon him, aspersions similar to those made by non-Muslims before (our time). We cannot absolve such folk simply because they do not know the Prophet, and we do not say, "If they only knew him, they would not do this." (All of this stems from not knowing the Prophet's rank.) For surely the one who does not believe in the Prophet's superiority, necessarily believes in the superiority of another over him, or the equality of another to him. Our concern is with the Muslim who does not know, or does not recognize, the rank of our Prophet. He may believe there is someone equal or better to (Muḥammad) al-Muṣṭafā, the chosen one.

My brothers in Islam, Almighty God is the one who has chosen the Prophet Muḥammad, peace and blessing be upon him, over the creation in the pre-eternity and the forever after. The plentiful testimony and evidence from the Qur'an and Ḥadīth are almost incalculable. By the will of God, we will cite some of them here, hoping to thereby clarify the truth for some of our youth intent on safeguarding their religion, whose thoughts are perhaps disrupted by current trends and events. We hope that they may remain steadfast and be assured that they are on the truth, that they walk on the straight path.

Is it possible to prefer some Prophets over others?

The Qur'ān is very clear in the case of preferring some Prophets over others, and that some Prophets are superior, for they have different ranks with God Almighty. This differentiation is either due to the level of the tribulations and adversities they bore in order to call to God, or simply due to divine preference bestowed upon them, which God can grant to whomever he wills. These two are the opinions of our established scholars who are firmly rooted in sacred knowledge. God says:

> *These Messengers: We favored some of them over others. God spoke directly to some of them and raised up some of them in rank. We gave Clear Signs to Jesus, son of Maryam, and reinforced him with the Holy Spirit. If God had willed, those who came after them would not have fought each other after the Clear Signs came to them, but they differed. Among them there are those who have faith and among them there are those who are non-believers. If God had willed, they would not have fought each other. But God does what He wills.*[179]

When Almighty God informs us that he preferred some Messengers (over others), He indicates some of the reasons for this preference by saying: "*God spoke directly to some of them and raised up some of them in rank. We gave Clear Signs to Jesus, son of Maryam*" and He also said "*We gave David the Psalms*"[180] and the Almighty also said: "*And We gave him (Jesus) the Gospel, and We gave Moses and Aaron the Criterion, light and remembrance for the righteous,*"[181] and He also said: "*We gave David and Solomon knowledge,*"[182] and He said: "*And we took the covenant from the Prophets, and from you (Muḥammad) and Noah.*"[183] Notice, in this last verse, He generalized the covenant to all the Prophets, and then he specified their names, beginning with Muḥammad, peace and blessing be upon him.

---

179 Qur'ān, 2:253.

180 Qur'ān, 17:55.

181 Qur'ān, 21:48.

182 Qur'ān, 27:15.

183 Qur'ān, 33:7.

Some students of sacred knowledge have been puzzled by some confirmed *ḥadīth*s of the Prophet Muḥammad, peace and blessings be upon him, such as: "Do not choose one Prophet over another, and do not make preferences among the Prophets of God". This *ḥadīth* was narrated by our most reliable Imams. Indeed, we do not say: "a certain person is better than another." The Prophet also said, peace and blessings be upon him, "One should not say that I am better than Yūnus b. Matā (Jonah, son of Amittai)."

The distinguished scholars have answered this question in two ways. First, the Qur'ān verses already mentioned abrogate the prohibitions of preference found in the *ḥadīth*. Moreover, the prohibition mentioned in the *ḥadīth* was said prior to the revelation about his preference over all others, and also prior to him knowing that he is the master (*sayyid*) of the children of Adam. It is well known that the sacred texts can sometimes abrogate one another. But in this case, it is impossible that the *ḥadīth* which states "I am the Master of the children of Adam" could be abrogated, for such would entail the demotion of the Prophet's rank, peace and blessing be upon him, and no Muslim would ever make that claim.

A second answer is that the Prophet said "Do not assign me superiority over Moses" out of humility. During his acceptance of the Caliphate upon the death of the Prophet, Abu Bakr said, "I will accept the leadership, but I am not the best of you". This was said out of humility, for everyone knew that Abu Bakr was indeed the best of them. Likewise, when the Prophet said, "One should not say that I am better than Jonah," he was saying that out of humility, for he was not known to boast. Indeed, when the Almighty said to the Prophet "do not be like the Companion of the Whale (*ḥūt*)," this suggests that the Prophet indeed had a preference over Jonah. This then leads to the conclusion that the *ḥadīth* "One should not say that I am better …" was said out of humility.

Some scholars said that it is prohibited for the laymen to debate the preferred ranks of the Prophets for it may lead to inappropriate discussion and compromise the respectable rank of the Prophets. In his Qur'an exegesis, Imam al-Qurtubī mentioned some directives regarding this matter:

The best of what was mentioned is that the prohibition of preference is solely regarding prophecy, which is the one matter on which we may not waiver. On the other hand, the preferences of Prophets lie in the rank of their conditions, unique attributes, nobility, grace, and manifested miracles. But as for prophethood in and of itself, we do not differentiate among the Prophets.

The ranking of Prophets is due to circumstances by which they were preferred. For this reason, some of the Prophets are Messengers, others are referred to as Arch Prophets (*awalū al-*ʿazm), and among them there are those whom God took as a close friend, while others spoke to God, and those who were raised in degrees.

God said: "*I have preferred some Prophets over others, and We gave David the Psalms.*" He also said: "*those Messengers, whom We preferred some over others.*"

The ranking of Prophets is based on their superiority granted on account of their virtues and by the custom of causal effects.[184] Ibn ʿAbbās highlighted this when he said: "God favored Muḥammad over all Prophets and the inhabitants of the Heavens (*ahl al-samāʾ*)." Those present then asked, "With what was he preferred over the inhabitants of the Heavens?" His response was, "God the Almighty said (to the denizens of the Heavens): '*If any of them should say, I am a God besides Him, such a one We should reward with Hell. Thus We punish the oppressors.*'[185] And to the Prophet Muḥammad, peace and blessings be upon him, God said: '*Truly We granted you a clear victory, so that God may forgive your previous errors and any later ones.*'"[186] Those present then asked: "With what was he preferred over Prophets? Ibn ʿAbbās replied, "God Almighty said (about the rest of the Prophets), '*We have only sent Messengers with the language of their people to explain to them,*'[187] and God said to Muḥammad, peace

184 In other words, God gives preference to whom He wills without cause, but also grants favor by way of secondary causes.

185 Qurʾān, 21:29.

186 Qurʾān, 48:1.

187 Qurʾān, 14:4.

> and blessings be upon him, '*And we have sent you to all people*,'[188] and (this means that) God sent him to both Jinn and (all of) humanity. This was mentioned by Abū Muḥammad in his *Musnad*. Abū Hurayra said: "The best of the sons of Adam are Noah, Abraham, Moses and Muḥammad, peace be upon him, for they are the Arch Prophets among the Messengers."

And the summation of all this is that both the Qur'ān and the Ḥadīth confirm the preference of Prophets over each other. This is the reason why the Prophet, peace and blessings be upon him, said "I am the noblest of the children of Adam," and he also said, "I am the master of the children of Adam".

The Superiority of the Prophet Muḥammad in the Qur'ān

Almighty God said:

> *Remember when God made a covenant with the Prophets: "Now that We have given you a share of the Book and Wisdom, and then a messenger comes to you confirming what is with you, you must then have faith in him and help him," God then asked, "Do you agree and undertake My commission on those conditions?" They replied, "We agree." He said, "Bear witness, then. I am with you as one of the witnesses."*[189]

He also said:

> *When We made a covenant with all the Prophets—with you (Muḥammad) and with Noah and Abraham and Moses and Jesus, son of Maryam—We made a binding covenant with them.*[190]

---

188 Qur'ān, 34:28.

189 Qur'ān, 3:81.

190 Qur'ān, 33:7.

Imam al-Qurṭubī said regarding this verse:

> God required that the Prophets proclaim that the Muḥammad is the Messenger of God, peace and blessings be upon him. And He also required that Muḥammad, peace and blessings be upon him, announce that there will be no Prophets after him.

In a *ḥadīth* narrated by Qatāda on the authority of Ḥasan on the authority of Abu Hurayra, the Messenger of God, peace and blessings be upon, was asked regarding the covenant verse just mentioned. His response was, "I was the first created and the last one sent". Imam Mujāhid said, "The Prophet was present in the loins of Adam," peace and blessing be upon him.

God Almighty said: *"If there comes to you a Messenger confirming what you have, you must believe in him and support him."*[191] Imam ʿAlī and Ibn ʿAbbās both stated that the specific Messenger referred to here is Muḥammad, peace and blessing be upon him. According to the Qur'ān exegesis of Ibn Kathīr,[192] (these same Companions) ʿAlī b. Abī Ṭālib and his cousin ʿAbdallāh b. ʿAbbās, may God be pleased with them, both said that God did not send a Prophet except by taking this covenant with them. The covenant was that if the Prophet was sent during their time, that they and their followers would believe in him and follow him.

The Superiority of the Prophet in the *Ḥadīth*

Imam Aḥmad narrated:

> On the authority of ʿAbd al-Razzāq, from Sufyan, from Jābir, from Shaʿbī, from ʿAbdallāh b. Thābit, who said: "ʿUmar came to the Prophet, peace be upon him and said: 'O Messenger of God, I passed a brother of mine from the tribe of Quraydha (a Jewish tribe of

191 Qur'ān, 3:81.

192 Ismāʿīl b. Kathīr (d. 1373, Damascus) was a prominent Shāfiʿī scholar and ḥadīth expert who authored a magisterial Qur'ān exegesis known as *Tafsīr Ibn Kathīr*.

> Madina), who wrote for me some verses from the Torah. May I share them with you?" The Prophet's face then changed, peace and blessing be upon him.
>
> The narrator then asked ʿUmar, "Did you hear the reaction of the Prophet?"
>
> ʿUmar replied, "We are well pleased with God as our Lord, Islam as our religion, and Muḥammad as His Messenger!"
>
> ʿAbdallāh b. Thābit then asked, "But tell me what the Messenger said to you."
>
> ʿUmar replied, "The Prophet said, 'In the Name of Him in whose hand is the soul of Muḥammad, if Moses were resurrected today, and you were to follow him and not me, you would be astray. You (Muslims) are my ordained portion from among all people and I am your portion from the Prophets.'"

Imam Abū Bakr[193] relates on the authority of Isḥāq, Ḥammād, Mujāhid, al-Shaʿbī, and Jābir who said:

> The Messenger of God, peace and blessings be upon him, said: "Do not ask the people of the Book about anything, for they will not guide you due to their misguidance. You will end up either believing in falsehood or disbelieving in the truth. For by God, if Moses were alive today, he would have no alternative but to follow me."

In another *ḥadīth*, he said: "If either Moses or Jesus were alive, they would have no option but to follow me." In his book *Ḥilyat (al-awliyā')*, Abū Naʿīm (al-Iṣfahānī)[194] related on the authority of Anas b. Mālik, may God be pleased with him, who said:

> The Messenger of God, peace and blessings be upon him, said, "God revealed to Moses, the Prophet of the children of Israel, that whoever

---

193 This appears to be a reference to Abū Bakr al-Ajurrī (d. 971, Baghdad), who authored a famous collection of forty *ḥadīth*. Among his students was Abū Naʿīm al-Iṣfahānī.

194 This widely read collection of reports about the Prophet's companions, written by Aḥmad Abū Naʿīm al-Iṣfahānī (d. 1038), provides evidence of the saintly qualities of the early Muslims.

comes before me with ingratitude towards Aḥmad will enter Hellfire."
Moses then asked, "My Lord, who is Aḥmad?'
God said, "I have not created anyone nobler than him. I wrote his name along with Mine on the Throne prior to the creation of the heavens and earth. None of my creation will enter Paradise except after he and his followers enter it."
Moses then asked, "Who are his followers?"
God said, "Those who praise God (*al-ḥāmidūn*), who praise God when mounting and dismounting, and in all their affairs. They stick to the middle course. They purify themselves. They fast during the day. They are monks by night. I will accept even the menial acts they do, and I will cause them to enter Paradise with (the statement), 'There is no god but God' (*la ilāh ill-Allāh*)."
Moses said, "Make me the Prophet of those people!"
God said, "Their Prophet is from among them."
Moses then said, "Make me from that Prophet's people!"
God said, "You have preceded him, and he will come after you, but I will join you with him in the Glorious Abode".

The Prophet, peace and blessings be upon him, said, "I was sent to the red and the black, and the earth was made a place of worship and a source of purification for me. Spoils of war were made permissible for me, and I was granted intercession for others."

The Prophet Muḥammad is the Seal of all Prophets, may the peace and blessings of God be upon him till the Day of Judgment. He is the greatest Imam, for if he were present at any time in human history obedience to him would take precedence over all other Prophets. And for this reason, he was the Imam of all the Prophets during the night journey to Jerusalem, when they all congregated at the Holy Mosque. It is also for this reason that he is the intercessor on the Day of Gathering when our Lord will bring forth His judgment. To the Prophet belongs the Praiseworthy Station (*maqām al-maḥmūd*). This befits only him, for it is a title which has been relinquished by all other Prophets, Messengers, and (even) the Arch Prophets. Prophethood ended with his appearance, so the title is exclusively his.

The Superiority of the Prophet's Followers

The Almighty said:

> *You are the best community ever brought forth among mankind. You enjoin the right, forbid the wrong, and have faith in God. If the people of the Book were to have faith, it would be better for them. Some of them are believers, but most of them are deviators.*[195]

It can be inferred from this verse that the Prophet Muḥammad, peace and blessings be upon him, is indeed preferred over his brothers among the Prophets, peace be upon them, and this results in the preference of this religious community (*umma*) due to his superiority, may the peace and blessings of God be upon him and his family. Ibn Kathīr states in his exegesis:

> This community has superiority over others due to its Prophet, peace and blessings be upon him, for he is the most honored of God's creations, and he is the most generous of all the noble Messengers. He was sent by God with the complete Law that which was not given to any Prophet or Messenger prior to him.

Imam al-Tirmidhī narrates on the authority of Bahz b. Hakīm, from his father, from his grandfather that he heard the Messenger of God, say, "When God said, 'You are the best community ever brought forth among mankind,' (it means that) you surpass and are more noble than seventy (other religious) communities."

This is the case whether it be the earliest Muslims of the community or the last of them. It was narrated that Muḥammad b. Abi Hamīd, from Zaid b. Aslam, from his father, from 'Umar who was reported to have said:

> I was sitting with the Messenger of God, peace and blessings be upon him, when he said, "Do you know who among the creation has the best faith?"

---

195 Qur'ān, 3:110.

> We responded, "The Angels?"
> He said, "It is indeed befitting them, but no."
> We then responded, "Then the Prophets?"
> He then said, "It is befitting them, but no."
> The Messenger of God, peace and blessings be upon him, said, "The best of creation in faith are a people who emerge from the loins of men, who believe in me though they have not seen me. They find direction from a written text, and they act according to it, for they have the highest faith."

It was narrated on the authority of Ṣāliḥ b. Jubayr, from Abu Jumʿa who said: "We asked, 'O Messenger of God, are there any people who are better than us?' He then replied 'Yes, people who come after you who will find a book between two covers, they will believe in what it contains, and they will believe in me though they have not seen me.'"

Just as God Almighty singled out his Prophet with the previously mentioned characteristics, He also singled out the Prophet's community, peace and blessings be upon him. For this community is a unique people, they are superior to all others. This community is the strongest in faith and certainty, and this faith is based on knowledge. The *ḥadīth* of the Messenger attest to this. It was narrated on the authority of Abu Naʿīm, from Abu Hurayra, may God be pleased with him, that the Messenger, peace and blessing be upon him, said:

> When the Torah was revealed to Moses, he found our community mentioned in it. He said to God, "I have found in the Tablets a nation that will come at the end of time who is superior to any other, so make it my community!"
> God said, 'That is the community of Aḥmad'.
> Moses then said, "I have also found that there is a community who preserves its revelation by memory and its people recite it openly, so make it my community!"
> God said, "That is the community of Aḥmad."
> Moses then said, "My Lord, I have found in the Tablets reference to a community that is permitted to take the spoils of war, so make it my community!"

> God said, "That is the community of Aḥmad."
> Moses then said, "I found reference in the Tablets to a community who gives and accepts charity, so make it my community!"
> God said, "That is the community of Aḥmad."
> Moses then said, "I have found reference in the tablets to a community that is rewarded for (even) contemplating a good deed, and if the good deed is carried out its people are rewarded ten-fold, so make it my community!"
> God said, "That is the community of Aḥmad."
> Moses then said, "I have found reference in the Tablets to a community, that if its people only contemplate a bad deed they do not incur a sin, but should they do it they only incur a single sin, so make it my community!"
> God said, "That is the community of Aḥmad."
> Moses then said, "I have found reference in the Tablets to a community whose members are given knowledge about the beginning and the end of time, and they will kill the Antichrist (*dajjāl*), so make it my community!"
> God said, "That is the community of Aḥmad."
> Moses then said, "Then my Lord make me from the community of Aḥmad!"
> It was then that Moses was granted his two distinctions and God then said, "O Moses, I have preferred you over people by giving you the Torah and by My speaking to you. Take what I have given you and be among those who are grateful."
> Moses then said, "I am well pleased, my Lord."

All of this refers to the community of our Prophet Muḥammad, peace and blessings be upon him. It was mentioned in the *Ḥilyat* on the authority of Anas b. Malik:

> Moses the son of ʿImran was walking on a road one day when he was called by the All-Powerful, "O Moses!" Moses then turned looking in each direction to no avail. He was then called a second time "O Moses, son of ʿImran!" Moses once again turned looking in each

direction to no avail. He was then called a third time, "O Moses son of Imran, I am God! There is no god but Me".

Moses then responded, "I am at your service, I am at your service!" and he immediately prostrated.

God then said, "Moses, son of ʿImran, raise your head." Moses complied. God then said, "Moses, if you desire to be in the shade of my throne, on the Day when there will be no shade except My shade, then be to the orphan as a merciful father, and be to the widow as a caring husband. O Moses, be merciful and you will be granted mercy. O Moses, you will be reciprocated according to your actions. O Moses son of ʿImrān, inform the children of Israel that whoever meets me after they have rejected Muḥammad I will cause them to enter Hellfire, even though Abraham is my friend (*khalīl*), and Moses is with whom I spoke (*kalīm*)."

Moses then asked, "Who is Muḥammad?"

God said, "By My Power and My Might, no one is nobler among My creation than him. I wrote his name along with My Name on the Throne a thousand years prior to creating the heavens, the earth, the sun, and the moon. By My Power and My Might, no one will enter Paradise until he and his community enter it."

Moses then said, "Who belongs to the community of Muḥammad?"

God said, "They are those who praise God (*al-ḥāmidūn*), whether mounting or dismounting, and in all their affairs. They stick to the middle course. They purify themselves. They fast during the day. They are monks by night. I will accept even the menial acts they do, and I will cause them to enter Paradise with (the declaration), 'There is no god but God' (*la ilāh ill-Allāh*)."

Moses then said, "Make me the Prophet of those people!"

God said, "Their Prophet is from among them."

Moses then said, "Make me from that Prophet's people."

God said, "You have preceded him, and he will come after you, but I will join you with him in the Glorious Abode."

It was also narrated by Ibn ʿAbbās:

> Moses said, "O Lord, is there any community that is superior to my community? You have shaded my people with clouds and sent down upon them manna and quails."
> God said, "O Moses, know that my preference for the community of Muḥammad over all other communities is as My superiority over all my creation."
> Moses then said, "My Lord, allow me to see them."
> God said, "You will not see them, but I will allow you to hear them".
> God then called this community, and they responded in unison, "We are at you service our Lord!"
> God said, "My peace and blessings are upon you. My mercy upon you will prevail over My anger, and My forgiveness will prevail over My punishment. I have answered your prayers before you ask Me. Whoever presents himself to Me while bearing witness, 'there is no god but God and Muḥammad is His Messenger,' I will forgive all of his sins."

The Prophet Muḥammad then said, "God decreed that these bounties are given to me." The reference to this dialogue is found in the verse, "*Nor were you on the side of the Mount when We called.*"[196]

Among the other distinctions of this community is that the legal rulings of the other communities ended at the death of their Messengers. But the Sacred Law (*sharīʿa*) of our Master Muḥammad, peace and blessings be upon him, will continue till the Day of Resurrection. This is unprecedented. Any Prophet who is resurrected after the coming of our Prophet must then follow him. Such is the case with Jesus, peace be upon him, as was mentioned by Imam al-Qurṭubī and others. Thus, when Jesus, peace be upon him, returns he will be following our Prophet's legal rulings, peace and blessings be upon him. And the case is likewise the same with Khiḍr, for those who believe that he is still alive. Both must follow the *Sharīʿa* of Muḥammad, peace and blessings be upon him, and they will never depart from it.

196 Qurʾān, 28:46.

The Creed of the People of the Sunna and the Congregation

The creed (ʿaqīda) of the people of the Prophetic example and the (Muslim) congregation (*ahl al-sunna wa al-jamāʿa*) is the belief that our master Muḥammad, peace and blessings be upon him, is superior to the entire creation. The author of *Jawharat al-tawḥīd*, Shaykh Ibrāhīm Laqānī stated: "He is the absolute best of all creation and there is no disagreement in this regard. Then the Prophets come after him in degrees, followed by the Angels."

In his commentary, Imam Al-Bayjūrī said the following about these lines: "The Prophet in his essence and in his character is the best of all creation whether they be in the heavens or on earth, whether they be among the Jinn or mankind, whether they be Angels in this world or the next." He further said, "His superiority over all creation is unanimously agreed upon by the majority of Muslim, even the Muʿtazila. He is then followed in ranks by the Angels and other people." Al-Zamakhsharī[197] diverged from this consensus by claiming that (the Angel) Gabriel is superior to the Prophet, but the scholars have refuted his claim. And while this platform does not afford us the time to review this particular divergence, you may refer to the literature if you so desire.

It was narrated that the Prophet said, "I am the most honored in the sight of God from among the first and the last of mankind, and I am not boasting." The reference to not boasting could either mean, "I am not saying this to boast, rather only stating a blessing," or it could mean, "there is nothing more worthy about which to boast."

Scholars have differed whether this superiority was granted to him due to his merit or simply due to the fact that God preferred him and placed him it that rank, peace and blessing be upon him. The most reliable opinion is that God has preferred our Prophet over the creation, not due to merit but through His Will. The Prophet's superiority was indeed granted to him as a merit, but such merit is not a prerequisite to his superiority.

---

197 Abū l-Qāsim Maḥmūd al-Zamakhsharī (d. 1143) was a Persian scholar of the Muʿtazilite school whose linguistic commentary on the Qur'ān, *al-Kashshāf ʿan ḥaqāʾiq al-tanzīl*, was considered a useful exegesis among the wider orthodox Muslim community.

As for Imam Laqānī stating that "the Prophets come after him in degrees," this means they follow him in superiority, peace and blessings be upon them. Therefore, they rank after him in degree, peace and blessing be upon them. Yet, they are not of equal rank. Rather, the order (after our master Muḥammad) is as follows: our master Abraham, then our master Moses, then our master Jesus, then our master Noah. These are the Arch Prophets, the possessors of determination, who endured much hardship. And following the Arch Prophets in rank are the rest of the Messengers, then the Prophets in their respective ranks with God. Following the Prophets are the Angels, the possessors of excellence, who are ranked after all the Prophets. The first Angels that follow the Prophets would be their leaders, Gabriel, Michael, Isrāfīl, and ʿAzrāʾīl, followed by the rest of the Angels. This is the Sunni creed as it has been transmitted to us.

The Most High said (concerning the Prophet), "*Truly, you are of tremendous character.*"[198] Ibn ʿAbbās and Mujāhid said "of character" (ʿala *khuluq*) means "of a great religion (*dīn*) among all religions." There is no religion more loved by God the Most High, and none more pleasing to Him. Indeed, according to Āʾisha in *Ṣaḥīh Muslim*, his character was the Qurʾān. She was asked another time concerning the character of the Prophet, peace on him. She recited the verses of the Qurʾān:

> *Successful indeed are the believers, who are humble in their prayers, those who shun vain conversation, those who pay the alms (zakāt), those who guard their chastity except from their wives or what their right hands possess, for then they are not blamed. But whoever craves what is beyond that, such are transgressors. But those who keep their trust and their pledge, and those who observe their prayers, they are the inheritors.*[199]

Then she said, "There was no one with a better character than the Messenger, God's peace and blessing upon him. Whenever one of his companions or family members called for him, he responded with 'at your service' (*labayk*). And that is why God the Most High said, 'Truly,

198 Qurʾān, 68:4.

199 Qurʾān, 23:1-10.

you are of tremendous character.'" And He did not mention any praiseworthy character except that it belonged to the Prophet, God's peace and blessing upon him. This was the most abundant provision from God.

Prophets Muḥammad, Abraham, and Moses

The essence of the matter is that our master Muḥammad, God's blessing and peace upon him, is the Seal and Imam of the Prophets. His religion is the best of religions. His community is the best of communities. His Book is the best of Books revealed from Heaven. His was the first fragrance inhaled by the earth. He is the first to enter the Garden. To him belongs the intercession. God's exaltation is on him who, by Him, was honored over all others. This exaltation belongs to him whose mention was raised high, to him who was given victory and forgiveness. It belongs to him whose family was purified from abomination, to him who was carried on the night journey, and by whose life, time-period, and homeland God swore oaths. It belongs to him who was given the Fountain of Abundance (*al-kawthar*), to him whose revelation (*ayāt*) have remained continuously with us, to him whose religion abrogated all other religions, to him who was sent to the entirety of creation.

If we were to speak of his position by comparing it to a position other than his among the Prophets, we would find that his is (most similar to) the position of (Prophet Abraham), the Friend (*al-Khalīl*, of God).

The station of Prophet Abraham, the Friend, was one desirous of forgiveness. "*And who, I ardently hope, will forgive my sin on the Day of Judgment.*"[200] The station of Prophet Muḥammad the Beloved in this affair was, "*We have indeed given you a manifest victory. That God may forgive you of your sin, that which is past and that which is to come.*"[201]

The station of Abraham the Friend was one of need, "*And disgrace me not on the day when they are raised.*"[202] And Muḥammad the Beloved was

200 Qur'ān, 26:82.

201 Qur'ān, 48:1-2.

202 Qur'ān, 26:87.

given more than his need, "*A day when God will not disgrace the Prophet and those with him.*"[203]

The Friend said, "*And give unto me a good report in later generations.*"[204] As for the Beloved, (God said), "*And we have exalted your mention.*"[205]

The Friend said, "*And turn me and my sons away from worshipping idols.*"[206] As for the Beloved, (God said), "*God only wants to remove abomination from you, O family of the Prophet (ahl al-bayt).*"[207]

The Friend said, "*Sufficient for me is God.*"[208] As for the Beloved, (God said) "*O Prophet, God is sufficient for you.*"[209]

The Friend said, "*I am going to my Lord, He will guide me.*"[210] As for the Beloved, (God said), "*Glory to Him who carried His servant by night.*"[211]

Concerning Moses, the one with whom God spoke, he came to the appointed place (at the burning bush). As for Muḥammad the Beloved: "*Glory be to Him who carried His servant...*"

The intimate discourse of Moses (with God) took place on the mountain. The intimate discourse of the Beloved took place beyond the Throne, and beyond the beyond.

God spoke with Moses, a revelation from Him (calling Moses) to Him Most High. God (also) spoke directly to Muḥammad, God's blessing and peace upon him.

God responded to Moses by saying, "*You will not see Me.*"[212] But God related concerning Muḥammad, peace and blessings upon him, "*The (Prophet's) heart in no way falsified what he saw.*"[213]

---

203 Qur'ān, 66:8.

204 Qur'ān, 26:84.

205 Qur'ān, 94:4.

206 Qur'ān, 14:35.

207 Qur'ān, 33:33.

208 Qur'ān, 39:38.

209 Qur'ān, 8:64.

210 Qur'ān, 37:99.

211 Qur'ān, 17:1.

212 Qur'ān, 7:43.

213 Qur'ān, 53:11.

Moses collapsed in a faint. As for the Beloved, *"His vision did not waver, nor did it stray."*[214]

God narrated His conversation with Moses, with such words as, *"What is that in your right hand, Moses."*[215] But He concealed and veiled His intimate conversation with the Beloved by saying, *"And He revealed to His servant what He revealed."*[216]

The Spiritual Reality of the Prophet Muḥammad[217]

God, may He be praised, has honored all of humanity with the existence of our master Muḥammad. He is the light of existence (*wujūd*), the spiritual assistance (*madad*) of existence. Indeed, he is the very substance of existence (*wujūd al-wujūd*), and there is no existence except his existence, and no light except his light, may God bless him and grant him peace. He is the master of "If not for you (I would not have created the creation)."[218] He said, "I am from the Light of God, and the believers are from my light." May God's blessings and peaceful salutations be upon him, on his family, and on his companions; those who sheltered him and helped him, and those who followed the Light sent down with him. These are God's group (*ḥizb*), surely the group of God are the felicitous ones.

He was the first appearance (*bāriz*) among the manifestations of the Real, glorious and exalted is He. In the *ḥadīth* we read (the words of God to the Prophet): "I was a hidden treasure, unknown, but I loved to be known. So I created the creation, and they came to know Me. So by Me, they know me." Our master Shaykh Ibrāhīm Niasse, may God be pleased with him, said that his light was the first of the existence to exist. He is the source (*aṣl*) of sources and the source of all (human) offspring.

---

214 Qur'ān, 53:17.

215 Qur'ān, 20:17.

216 Qur'ān, 53:10.

217 This section is inserted from a speech delivered for the celebration of the Prophet (*mawlid*) in Kumasi, Ghana, on April 25, 2014. The selection here represents roughly one half of the original Arabic.

218 This is a famous *ḥadīth* relating the words of God to the Prophet Muḥammad, a *ḥadīth* authenticated by, among others, Ibn Taymiyya in his *Majmaʿ fatāwa*.

By him, God's blessing and peace on him, we became the best of communities brought forth for mankind.

We know for certain, all of us, that he is the best of the creation without exception. He said: "When God created this world, He created the heavens, and made of them seven and stabilized them. He created the earth, and made seven of it, and caused to dwell on it whomever He wills of His creation. He created the creations, and He chose among them the children of Adam. From the children of Adam, He chose the Arabs. From the Arabs, He chose the Quraysh. From the Quraysh, He chose Maḍar. From (the descendants of) Maḍar, He chose the Banū Hāshim. From the Banū Hāshim, He chose me. I have been selected from the best people among the best people. Whoever loves the Arabs, loves them because he loves me, and whoever hates them hates me."

In the book, *Dalāʾil al-nubuwwa* of Abū Naʿīm (al-Iṣfahānī), is found the following description of the Prophet: "He is the eraser (*al-māḥī*), the gatherer (*al-ḥāshir*), the successor (*al-*ʿāqib), the exemplar (*al-maqfī*), the Prophet of mercy, the Prophet of repentance, the Prophet of martial valor (*malāḥim*), a mercy, a guidance, a blessing, a benefit, the one chosen (*al-muṣṭafa*), the luminous lamp (*al-sirāj al-munīr*)."

It has been related in the *ḥadīth* collections of al-Bukhārī, Muslim and al-Tirmidhī that Jubayr b. Muṭʿim said, "I heard the Messenger of God, blessing and peace upon him, say: 'I have many names. I am Muḥammad. I am Aḥmad. I am the eraser by whom God erases disbelief (*kufr*). I am the most praised. I am the gatherer around whose feet the people will gather. I am the successor (of the Prophets), and there is no prophet after me.'"

The abundance of names is evidence of the honor for the one named. The praise poets have indeed praised him with all manners of praise down through the generations. Imam al-Buṣayrī said in his *Burda*:

His birth revealed the purity of his ancestry
How pure his origin, how pure his final end![219]

---

219 Muḥammad al-Buṣayrī, *al-Burda al-sharīf,* line 59. I have borrowed the translation here of Abdal Hakim Murad, *The Mantle Adorned* (Quilliam Press, 2009), 75.

The poet Shawqī said:

> Your brother Jesus called to a dead person, who stood up for him
> You gave life to all who came forth out of nonexistence.

Imam Nabahānī said:

> Your light is everything, and the rest of mankind is but parts
> O my Prophet! The rest of the Prophets are among his soldiers.

Our master (Ibrāhīm Niasse), the bringer of the great Tijānī flood, may God be pleased with him, said:

> Muḥammad is the servant of God, there is none like him
> By him were enemies shredded with pebbles he threw.

And he said:

> You could say, "servant of God, and master (*sayyid*) of His creation"
> So say of him whatever you will, you would not exhaust his laudation.

And he said:

> The Seal of Prophets is superior
> To all the Messengers through God's personal address[220]
> The secret ocean, the praised one
> The sun of guidance and emulation.

This is Muṣṭafā, the chosen one, may God's peace and blessing be upon him. We must become enlightened with his lights and his character, and we must illuminate our lives and our affairs by him. We should beautify our

220 Elsewhere in *Nujūm al-hūdā*, Shaykh Ibrāhīm explained that the Prophet Muḥammad, unlike all other Prophets, was honored in the Qur'an by God's addressing him, "O Prophet of God" and various other epithets instead of being called directly by name, as in "O Moses!".

characters by him, all becoming those who love for their brothers what they love for themselves. The Prophet, the blessings and peace of God on him, said, "The Muslim is the brother of the Muslim: he does not wrong him, he does not take what belongs to him, he does not scorn him." (And in the Qur'ān) *"Surely the Messenger of God is a beautiful example."*[221]

We ask God Most High that He gather us in the company of the Prophet Muḥammad, and that He not prevent us from smelling his fragrance, and that He make us among those who know and grant recognition to his worth.

O God, bless our master Muḥammad, the opener of what was closed, the seal of what came before, the helper of the Truth with the truth, the guide to Your straight path, and on his family, (may this prayer) be commensurate with his rank, for great are the dimensions of his reality.

May the Peace, Mercy, and Blessing of God the Most High be with you.

---

221 Qur'ān, 32:21.

5.

Exemplary Etiquette between the Sacred Law and the Divine Reality

Lecture Delivered at the Diyanet Center of America, Lanham, Maryland (2017)

In the Name of God, the Compassionate the Merciful.

All praise to God who entrusted the children of Adam with the most excellent virtues, the most honorable attributes, the most praiseworthy elocution. (Praise to Him) who made ascendant nobility in the acquisition (of virtue) and not by familial attribution: "All of you are from Adam and Adam is from dust."

Blessings and peace on him who was sent to perfect the most honorable character traits, and upon his family and companions; (blessings) with each sudden illumination of the dawn.

May God the Most High be pleased with the hidden succor (*ghawth*), the renowned seal of Muḥammadan sainthood, our master Abū l-ʿAbbās Shaykh Aḥmad al-Tijānī, who quenched the thirst of his followers and beloveds with the greatest gentleness.

May (God's) mercy and pleasure be upon the one who transcended nationalities, who with his (divine) proximity provided the gnostics with delight and intimacy. And from the elixir of his spiritual training (*tarbiya*), quenched his disciples' thirst with the greatest courtesy: the axial saint of his age, the unique of his time, Abū Isḥāq Shaykh Ibrāhīm Niasse.

Surely the topic we are here addressing—plumbing its depths, plunging into its secrets—is of the utmost importance and intense preeminence. It is the heart of righteous deeds. It is the shield against excess. It is the foundation from which a person reaps righteousness from his deeds, and excellence from his actions, in both worldly affairs and religious affairs. Our subject is thus: "Etiquette with the Sacred Law and the Divine Reality".

We hope that this discussion of ours will comprehend the subject's inner realities and related tangents: for etiquette (*adab*) is the essential prerequisite of positive disposition (*shīma*), and the foundation of everything of value, and the cause of an honorable life. So (the good of) what I say is by God.[222]

---

222 In a subsequent paragraph in the Arabic original (missing from this translation), the Shaykh goes on to define the meaning of *adab* in Arabic, being related to words having to do with hosting a feast or inviting others to a laden table.

The Etiquette of the Prophet, God's blessing and peace on him

The Prophet, upon him blessing and peace, said: "My Lord trained me with the best refinement." Another way of saying, "My Lord trained me (*addabanī*)", would be to say, "My lord taught me discipline of the self (*riyādat al-nafs*) and the best of character traits (*akhlāq*), externally and internally." Etiquette (*adab*) is what the self obtains of good character traits and acquired knowledge. "The best refinement" is to say, "By His favor upon me with acquired and inspired knowledge, never before witnessed among humankind."

Some of have also said (of this *ḥadīth*) that it means he was trained with the etiquette of worshipful devotion (*ādāb al-ʿubūdiyya*) and adorned with the character of divinity (*akhlāq al-rabūbiyya*).

Al-Qurṭubī said: "God protected the Prophet, God's blessing and peace upon him, from his youth, and Himself took charge of the Prophet's refinement. God did not entrust anyone else for any portion of that, and He continued in this way until He had purified the Prophet from the states of pagan ignorance (*jāhiliyya*) and guarded him from them, so that he had nothing to do with such ignorance. All of that was God's grace and affection for him; and all good character traits became gathered in him."

In this manner did the Mother of Believers ʿĀʾisha, may God the Exalted be pleased with her, describe the Prophet, God's blessing and peace upon him, in the *ḥadīth* narrated by Muslim: "His character was the Qurʾān." In his Qurʾān exegesis, Ibn Kathīr said of this *ḥadīth*: "He became, God's blessing and peace upon him, the exemplar (*imtithāl*) of the Qurʾān, in both its commands and prohibitions. The Qurʾān was his innate disposition (*sajiyya*) and his character. What the Qurʾān commanded he performed, what it prohibited he left aside. Thus did God mold him with exalted character, with modesty, generosity, courage, forgiveness, forbearance, and every beautiful character trait."

According to ʿĀʾisha, may God be pleased with her, the Prophet used to supplicate, "O God: just as You have beautified my form, so beautify my character." This was narrated by Aḥmad (b. Ḥanbal) and his narration is reliable.

Abū Hurayra, may God be pleased with him, also related that the Prophet, peace and blessing upon him, used to pray, "O God, I seek refuge in You from dissension, hypocrisy and bad character traits." This was narrated by Abū Dāwud and al-Nasāʾī.

Who follows the merits of the best of creation (*sayyid al-wujūd*) will attain the fullest realization (of his religion). For he, prayer and peace upon him, is *the madrasa* of etiquette, restraint, graceful character, noble deeds, and exalted virtues. He used to avert his gaze, and he did not fixate on things. For the most part, his glance took notice of things, but he did not stare when he looked. His gaze was more often on the ground than in the heavens. When he walked with his companions, he let them lead him and did not precede them. He was the first to greet another person with peace. The world and all its belongings did not distress him. He did not get upset or seek to overcome others for his own sake. If he became angry, he turned and looked away. If he was happy, he lowered his gaze. The greater portion of his laughing was smiling, and then his teeth were like white shining hailstones. He shared with his companions in their everyday talk. If they mentioned worldly matters, he discussed that with them. If they mentioned the afterlife, he also discussed that with them. If they mentioned food or drink, he discussed that as well. He never found fault in any food presented to him. If it pleased him, he ate it. If it did not please him, he left it alone.[223]

---

223 The next 6-7 pages of the Arabic original go on to mention the Prophet's etiquette with children, his sewing his own clothes, his patience with people (even one who urinated inside the mosque). The Prophet was never the first to withdraw his hand from another. There is also substantial discussion of eating habits: eating and drinking with the right hand (except in the case of injury or acceptable excuse), washing hands before and after eating, discussion of food, praying for hosts, the preference of eating with three fingers (although a spoon is also acceptable), not reclining while eating, not addressing someone while eating except for necessary, not blaming food. There is also discussion of the *adab* of the gathering of people: seeking permission to enter, not to knock on the door with violence, taking permission to leave, giving greetings of peace when leaving, giving space for the person who enters a gathering, and keeping the trust of the gathering (not relating confidential information outside).

The role of religious education in acquiring etiquette

There is no better way to acquire and remain continually committed to etiquette other than religious education (*al-tarbiya al-dīniyya*). This is the method by which virtues are implanted in the souls of students, by which the roots of vice and depravity are plucked out, and the educated become habituated to exalted matters, endowed with heavenly character and exemplary fundamentals. As al-Mutanabbī[224] said: "In time, every man comes to possess that with which has become his habit."

Such moral education (*tarbiya*) possesses a certain *Sharīʿa*-based exhortation in Islam, for it is the path to reward and punishment, as well as learning. (And training begins) even from the naming of children, for it is encouraged to select for them good, pleasing names.

The educator plays an extraordinarily important role in the enactment of moral training (*tarbiya*), for according to his method the child will acquire awareness and praiseworthy habits. The child takes his teacher as a good example, imitates his actions, and copies his righteous deeds. The son cannot be steadfast in righteousness without the steadfast righteousness of the father. God the Exalted said:

> *The wall belonged to two young orphans in the town and there was buried treasure beneath it belonging to them. Their father had been a righteous man, so your Lord intended them to reach maturity and then dig up their treasure as a mercy from your Lord. I did not do [these things] of my own accord: these are the explanations for those things you could not bear with patience.*[225]

The father had died while the children were still young, or perhaps he died before their birth, according to God's will, exalted and majestic is He. So, it became necessary for them to attain maturity and become strong before

---

224 Aḥmad b. al-Ḥusayn al-Mutanabbī (d. 965) was a renowned Arab poet during the Abbasid Caliphate in Iraq. Aside from Iraq, he also lived for a time in Syria and Egypt.

225 Qur'ān, 18:82. Here the divinely inspired teacher of Moses, named Khiḍr according to Islamic tradition, explains to his traveling companion Moses why he rebuilt an identified wall in a town of miscreants: an apparently charitable act to an undeserving people.

bringing forth their treasure. However, their father did not train them, nor exert effort in raising them. But because he was a righteous servant of God, his children were in the custody of divine providence. Thus, God the Exalted says: "*Let those who would fear for the future of their own helpless children, if they were to die, show the same concern [for orphans]; let them reverence God and speak the truth.*"[226] This is a reminder to every parent that the reverence of God (*taqwā*) and speaking the truth can suffice one's children, even if the children are left helpless, removed from their parents. Then God the Praised and Exalted takes charge of their affairs after their parents, as a reward for their pious reverence and their speaking the truth.

Spiritual Training and Etiquette with God

The desired goal of spiritual training (*al-tarbiya al-rūḥiyya*), itself the cream of religious education and character formation, is the (self's) transformation from an impure soul (*nafs*) to a purified soul, from an unjust intellect to a divinely directed intellect (*ʿaql sharʿī*), from a heart inhabited by heedless frivolity and filth to a heart of peace and serenity, from a spirit wandering distracted from God, unaware and unfulfilled in its divine devotion, to a spirit cognizant of God, fulfilling the rights of devotion due to Him.

Among the definitions of etiquette among the Sufis was that proposed in Suhrawardi's *al-ʿAwārif*:[227] "Etiquette is the refinement of the external and the internal being, and if the servant's external being is refined, his internal state attains proper comportment (*ṣāra adīban*)." And it is narrated in *al-ʿAwārif* from ʿAbdallāh b. Mubārak:[228] "Etiquette (*adab*) is the knowledge of self (*nafs*)." Shaykh Tāj al-Dīn Ibn ʿAṭā-Allāh, may God the Exalted have mercy on him, said in *Liṭāʾif al-minan*:

---

226 Qurʾān, 4:9.

227 ʿUmar Suhrawardi (d. 1234, Baghdad), an ethnically Kurdish Sufi scholar in Iraq, expanded and formalized the Suhrawardiyya Sufi order. His book *ʿAwārif al-maʿārif* become a popular text within Sufism more broadly.

228 ʿAbdallāh b. Mubārak (d. 797, Khorasan) was a respected jurist and ḥadīth scholar known for his asceticism and piety.

> I heard out Shaykh Abū l-ʿAbbās al-Mursī, may God be pleased with him, say: "This saying ['Whoever knows himself knows his Lord'][229] has two interpretations. The first is that whoever knows his own lowliness, helplessness and poverty, he will come to know God in His glorious might, power, and self-sufficiency. Thus, he comes to know himself first, and knows God thereafter. The second is that whoever knows himself must have already known God. The first interpretation refers to the state of the spiritual seekers (*sālikīn*), the second refers to the state of the divinely enraptured (*majdhūbīn*)."

Ibn ʿAṭā-Allāh also said, "Etiquette is stopping with what is appropriate (*waqūf maʿa l-mustaḥsanāt*)." He was asked, "What does that mean?" He said, "That your relationship with God, secretly and openly, is based on proper comportment (*adab*); then you will become a person of refinement (*adīb*)."[230] Then he recited the verses:

> When she spoke, she manifested all beautiful pleasantry
> And when she was silent, she manifested all pleasant beauty

The book *Bughyat al-mustifīd*[231] contains the following (relevant) quotation:

> The gist of such expressions that the consummate guides, may God be pleased with them, have presented in explanation of the reality of etiquette returns to the following notion. The purpose of etiquette is to beautify the state of the servant in what is between him and God the Exalted, between him and God's Angels, His books, His messengers, and all of humanity according to their differences of rank and type.

---

229 Reference to this section of the *Laṭāʾif* indicates "Whoever knows himself knows his Lord" is the ḥadīth under discussion in this passage. See Ibn ʿAṭā-Allāh al-Iskandarī, *The Subtle Blessings in the Saintly Lives of Abu al-Abbas al-Mursi and his Master Abu al-Hasan* (trans Nancy Roberts, Louisville, Kentucky: Fons Vitae, 2005), 54-55.

230 In some narrations, the quotation continues here, "... even if you are a non-Arab (*ʿajamī*)."

231 The book *Bughyat al-mustafīd sharḥ munyat al-murīd*, was written in the late nineteenth century by the Moroccan Tijānī scholar Muḥammad al-ʿArabī b. al-Sāʾiḥ. Ibn al-Sāʾiḥ was one of the most renowned leaders of the Tijāniyya in the nineteenth century, and his book has become a seminal text summarizing the practice and ideas of the Tijāniyya.

This is also mentioned by Shaykh Muḥyī al-Dīn (Ibn al-ʿArabī), may God be pleased with him, as the four types of etiquette. But in reality, these four can be condensed to two types: the etiquette of the jurists and the etiquette of the Sufis. The first is found within the second, as was clarified in *Jawāhir al-maʿānī*,[232] where [al-Tijānī's] words, may God have mercy on him, were as follows:

> Etiquette among the jurists is an expression of righteous deeds (*qiyām*) following what is legally obligatory and the example of the Prophet. These include deeds of excellence and those strongly encouraged pertaining to the (external) states of people, whether while sleeping, awake, eating or drinking, in remembrance and in supplication, and things like this. Among the Sufis, etiquette is an expression of all acquired virtue and piety. It is the description of all noble attributes and praiseworthy character traits related to divine adoration and the exaltation of divinity. Whoever gathers such traits in himself becomes refined and well-mannered in the presence of God the Exalted, and in the presence of His messenger, God's peace and blessing upon him. The first (juristic) meaning of etiquette is thus contained within the second.

We thereby come to understand that the previous *ḥadīth* in which the Prophet said, "My Lord educated me with the best refinement, and then decreed for me the most noble character," is the comprehensive foundation for all of these explanations. Etiquette is the gathering of all noble character traits and righteous deeds, the perfection of (human) attributes and correction of defects to the extent possible, fulfilling the rights of God and His servants, both individually and collectively. This latter is limited by the boundaries of the sacred law, for there can be no sense of propriety or refinement with the general population when such distances oneself from God the Exalted, *"even though they believe themselves to be doing good."*[233]

---

232 The *Jawāhir al-maʿānī wa bulūgh al-amānī*, was written around 1799 by Shaykh Aḥmad al-Tijānī's leading student, ʿAlī Ḥarāzim al-Barāda of Fez, Morocco. It contains the teachings of al-Tijānī and was approved from the Shaykh during his own lifetime, thus constituting the most important primary source of the Tijāniyya.

233 Qur'ān, 18:104.

The Sphere of training and purification in this Tijānī Muḥammadan Path

Our Shaykh Aḥmad al-Tijānī, may God be pleased with him, laid great stress on retreat (*khalwa*), silence (*ṣamṭ*) and withdrawal (from creation) and other things mentioned in the pure Prophetic example (*sunna*) [relating to the purification the *nafs*].[234] Among his exhortations in this regard was a letter he wrote to some of the jurists (*fuqahā'*) of Zarhūn[235] in response to their having written him:

> You mentioned the difficulty of fettering (*inqiyād*) your carnal self (*nafs*) to God's command, and of persisting in overcoming its unpleasantries. Indeed, this is a general rule God has established in the creation: that whoever should overlook his *nafs* and let it chase after its desires, the path to fulfilling God's command will be made difficult for him. Rather, let him see nothing in his *nafs* except viciousness, disobedience, and refusal of God's command. Who would rectify the screaming tantrums (*a'wijāj*) of his *nafs*, let him occupy himself with taming (*qam'*) his *nafs*, restricting it from the pursuit of its lusts. This is accomplished with persistent withdrawal ('uzla) from the creation, with silence, with lessening the intake of food, with incrementally increasing the remembrance of God, and with making the heart present to the remembrance (*dhikr*). The heart should be held back from plunging into its habitual distractions among the affairs of the world, held back from indulging in the world and loving it. The heart should be restrained from all volition, choice, planning, and from [seeking] information of the creation. Let the heart be bridled with the command of God, free of all anxiety. By persisting in this way, the *nafs* is purified, and it escapes from wickedness to conformity with the command of God. There is no other way than this. "*This*

234 This follows a lengthy section passed over in this truncated translation, explaining the Tijāniyya's emphasis on worldly involvement and avoiding the extreme acts of worldly renunciation associated with some Sufi communities.

235 This is a reference to Mt. Zarhūn in Morocco, or the town of Mawlay Idris I, one of the oldest Muslim settlements in Morocco.

> *is the way of God as it has been in the past, and you will not find any change in the way of God.*"[236]

Every station (*manzil*) along the path of religious development (*maqāmāt al-dīn*) requires its own etiquette, known by those who have realized this station.[237] Spiritual training thus depends, in its very essence, on etiquette with God the Exalted, both externally and internally. When wayfaring (*sulūk*) combines all types of etiquette and striving for perfection, it becomes the basis for arrival in divine presence, and the path is made easy. This is the path of endowment with excellent virtues, and purification from moral depravities. The Sufis say that etiquette is the only means by which the (true) seeker can be distinguished from others. The etiquette of the Sufis is that which connects them to the divine reality (*al-ḥaqīqa*) and allows them to benefit from this reality. It is not other than the Sacred Law (*sharīʿa*), for the *sharīʿa* with them is worship (*ʿibāda*), while the *ḥaqīqa* is loving devotion (*ʿubūdiyya*). The *sharīʿa* is adherence (*taʿalluq*), the path (*ṭarīqa*) is moral formation (*takhalluq*), the *ḥaqīqa* is actualization (*taḥaqquq*). Or you might say that *sharīʿa* is the door, the *ṭarīqa* is refinement (*ādāb*), and the *ḥaqīqa* is the essence; or that the *sharīʿa* is implementing divine commands, while the *ḥaqīqa* is etiquette and love in the presence of the command.

For Shaykh Ibrāhīm (Niasse), may God be pleased with him, the beginning of his spiritual training was being righteously steadfast (*istiqāma*) both externally and internally. He said:

> Who desires to be with me in my spiritual state, he must walk my path in both word and deed, implementing the commands and avoiding the prohibitions, externally and internally. And this while ardently longing to attain the pleasure of God and His Messenger.

In such respect, the Shaykh, may God be pleased with him, encouraged working to clean the lower self (*nafs*) from the stain of otherness (than

236 Ḥarāzim, *Jawāhir al-maʿānī*, II: 99. The Qur'an verse cited is 48:23.

237 Here the Shaykh, in the full document, goes on to mention the nine steps of spiritual wayfaring (repentance, steadfastness, fear, sincerity, truthfulness, serenity, observation, witnessing, and gnosis) and the different etiquette required of each.

God) until one had become a vessel, to the extent possible, containing the attributes of perfection. He said in one letter: "I advise all those who claim a state (of intimacy) with God, to persist in the struggle to purify the lower self, lest this self should say to him that he has arrived to a station exempt from work."

By this spiritual training, consisting of struggling against the lower self and restraining it from disobedience and from seeing other than God, by this does the aspirant arrive to illumination (*fatḥ*). The Shaykh al-Islam (Ibrāhīm Niasse) described such illumination as "a holy breath that pulls the servant's heart to the divine presence." He emphasized, "So long as the aspirant remains struggling and purifying himself from base character traits, his illumination comes to abide with him. But if he should shrug off (such work), he will return to darkness, and become like the man who saw something he liked in a dream but then woke up."

The aspirant should thus understand that etiquette — with God and with the guide who is the means to God, and with all of humanity, especially one's brethren in God — is the confluence of all perfection. It is the means by which spiritual states are corrected. The great scholar Ibn ʿAjība[238] said in his Qur'ān exegesis:

> The best of addresses is that by which etiquette is perfected. The perfection of etiquette is the cause of attaining that which is proper. Whoever has no etiquette has no training (*tarbiya*). Whoever has no training has no spiritual wayfaring. Who has no wayfaring has no arrival. Thus, whoever has no training by the hands of distinguished folk (*rijāl*) cannot be elevated among the distinguished.

The Sufi people have said, "The worst etiquette among the beloveds is to push away others from the door. And the worst etiquette (among the elite) is to push those at the door into bestial politics." Others have said, "Make your deeds pleasing, and your etiquette refined." Another said, "Mankind can achieve great ranks with good character and

238 Aḥmad Ibn ʿAjība (d. 1809, Morocco) was a renowned saint and scholar of the Darqawiyya-Shādhiliyya Sufi order.

comportment, even if his good deeds are few." Whoever is deprived of etiquette has been deprived of all good. Whoever is given etiquette has become among the keys of the hearts. Abū Ḥafṣ al-Ḥaddād,[239] may God be pleased with him, said:

> All of Sufism is etiquette. Every time has an etiquette. Every state has an etiquette. Every spiritual station (*maqām*) has an etiquette. Whoever persists in etiquette, attains what the distinguished folk have attained. Whoever is deprived of etiquette is distant (from God) even though he thinks himself close. He is rejected even though he hopes for arrival.

Dhū l-Nūn al-Miṣrī,[240] may God be pleased with him, said, "Whenever the aspirant neglects etiquette, he is returned to whence he came." And it is said, "Whoever has no etiquette for a time, that time of his becomes odious." And it is said, "Whoever measures himself by lineage, etiquette divorces him, and who has little etiquette has much unrest." And it is said, "Etiquette is the support of the poor, and the delight of the wealthy."

Many (of the righteous forefathers) used to say to their children: "O my son, for you to learn one door of etiquette is more loved to me than if you should learn seventy doors of knowledge." And Abū Ḥanīfa[241] said, "Hearing stories from the scholars is preferable to me than lots of jurisprudence; for they contain the etiquette and character of the exemplary folk."

May God the Exalted and Majestic make us among those whom He has educated with the best of refinements.

---

239 Abū Ḥafṣ ʿAmar al-Ḥaddād (d. 879) was a Sufi from Nishapur, Persia, who visited Junayd and al-Shiblī in Iraq. He was associated with the *Malāmatiyya* school of Sufism.

240 Dhū l-Nūn Thawbān al-Miṣri (d. 859) was an early Egyptian Sufi known for his elaboration of gnosis (*maʿrifa*).

241 Abū Ḥanīfa al-Nuʿmān (d. 767, Baghdad) was an early jurist and founder of the Ḥanifī school of law, the most popular in the Sunni Muslim world today.

6.

Sainthood in Islam and the Seal of Saints

Address delivered in Abidjan, Ivory Coast (2013)

Praise to God, who distinguished His saints (*awliyāʾ*) with the light of friendship (*walāya*), proximity to Him, and honored servitude in the spirit of the divine will. He has overwhelmed them in the flooding oceans of His blessings and secrets with the purest grace and generosity. He has guarded them with His protection, in the eye of providential care.

Blessing and peace on our Master Muḥammad, the source of sainthood. He who brought forth the treasure trove of secrets from the unseen, the witness. Peace on his family and companions for their role in giving righteous guidance. Peace on the successive generations of Muslims until the Day of Judgment.

May God's pleasure be on our master, the pole of the saintly poles, Aḥmad b. Maḥammad al-Tijānī, and on his inheritor (*khalīfa*) at every condition and degree of this Tijānī Sufi path, Shaykh Ibrāhīm b. al-Hajj ʿAbdallāh Niasse.

I turn my peace, greetings, and supplication to this blessed gathering, this protected place. This gathering is one that has congregated for the sake of God, blessed and exalted, not for any other reason. May God reward everyone with abundant goodness and protect you all with His eye of providential care, which never sleeps. And I say to you all: may God's peace, mercy, and blessing be on you.

The subject of our talk today, on this heavenly occasion, is a subject of utmost importance. The Seal of Muḥammadan Sainthood (*khatm al-walāya al-Muḥammadiyya*) possesses linguistic traces, perspectives, meanings, and established realities that the trifling winds cannot disturb, nor the tempests and sandstorms shake, due to the position's honor and exaltedness. This subject is an ocean. Only the fortunate one, granted Divine success, is able to plunge to its depths and bring forth its pearls and precious coral. This is my explanation of the topic, and with God is the success, for He is the guide by His favor on the straight path.

Understanding Sainthood

The word 'sainthood' (*walāya*) is derived from the word 'amity' or 'devotion' (*walāʾ*), so the meaning is close proximity (*qurb*). But there are two types of sainthood: general (*ʿāma*) and special (*khāṣṣa*). General sainthood is shared between all believers. God said, "*God is the Friend (Wālī) of those who believe, guiding them from the darkness to the light*" (Qur'an, 2:257). Special sainthood belongs to the elite, reserved for those who have arrived (in the Divine presence) among the masters of spiritual wayfaring (*sulūk*).

Special sainthood is an expression of the servant's annihilation (*fanāʾ*) in the Real, and his remaining (in the world) by Him. The saint is the one annihilated in Him, and the one remaining by Him. 'Annihilation' is an expression of the end of the journey *to* God. 'Remaining' (*baqāʾ*) is an expression of the beginning of the journey *in* God. The journey *to* God does not end until one has extinguished the desert of existence with the footstep of truthfulness. The journey *in* God does not begin until after the actualization of absolute annihilation. Then God gives him an existence bestowed (by Him), and a bodily presence (*dhāt*) pure of all filth. In this existence, he becomes described by God's descriptions, and his character becomes inculcated with God's characteristics. So now we read the *ḥadīth* (where God said), "I was a hidden treasure, and I wanted to be known. So I created the creation, and by Me they know Me." We also read in the *ḥadīth* (where God said), "My servant does not cease approaching Me with supererogatory good works until I love him, and when I love him, I become him."[242] This Divine 'becoming' (*kuntiyya*) is the essence of sainthood. Among the conditions of being a saint is being protected (*maḥfūẓ*), just as among the conditions of being a Prophet is being infallible (*maʿṣūm*). Sainthood has ranks, stations, and degrees, by which God distinguishes whom He wills with what He wills, and there is no end to His wisdom.

Knowing the Saint

Shaykh al-Imām Sīdī Yūsuf b. Ismāʿīl al-Nabahānī gave the following definition for the saint: "He is the one whose obedience has progressed (*tawālī*), removing him from being placed in disobedience." In other

---

242 This is an abbreviated rendition of the *ḥadīth*, often cited by Sufis, of a more widely circulated version in *al-Bukhārī* and elsewhere: "... when I love him, I become the hearing with which he hears, his seeing with which he sees, his hand with which he strikes, and his foot with which he walks."

words, the Real, glorious and exalted, takes possession (*yatawalla*) of him: protecting him, guarding him, moving him continuously away from all sorts of disobedience, and granting him enduring success in obedience. So this name (for saint, *walī*) is taken from the words of God: "*God is the Friend (Wālī) of those who believe,*"[243] and the Exalted's words: "*He is the protecting friend of the righteous.*"[244] Similar to this is the statement of the Most High, "*(O God) You are our Protecting Lord (mawlāna), so give us victory over the disbelieving people.*"[245] And the Most High said, "*That is because God is the Protecting Lord (Mawlā) of those who believe, and because those who do not believe, no protector have they.*"[246] And the Most High said, "*Indeed your protector is God and His Messenger.*"[247]

I would add that the linguistic meaning of the word "saint" here is proximity. If the servant is close to the presence of God on account of an abundance of obedience and sincerity, surely the Lord is close to him on account of His mercy, grace, and ultimate goodness. This is how sainthood is obtained. This was how Shaykh Ibrāhīm Niasse rooted the meaning in God's mighty book, for the Most High said, "*None but the reverent are its guardians (awliyā').*"[248] And the Most High said, "*Surely the saints of God are not beset by fear, nor do they grieve. They are those who have believed and were reverent.*"[249]

By this we understand that the saint is the one who reverences God. The reverence of God (*taqwa*), according to the Seal of Saints Shaykh Aḥmad al-Tijānī, may God be pleased with him and us on account of him, is nothing but implementing God's commands and avoiding His prohibitions, externally and internally, with what pleases Him and not with what pleases you.

---

243 Qur'ān, 2:257.

244 Qur'ān, 7:196.

245 Qur'ān, 2:286. In Arabic, the word *mawlā* or *mawlay* contains the same root *w-l-y* as the word for *walī* (saint, friend).

246 Qur'ān, 47:11.

247 Qur'ān, 5:55.

248 Qur'ān, 8:34. The reference here is to those tasked with guarding the sacred mosque (*ka'ba*) in Mecca.

249 Qur'ān, 10:62-63.

Reflections from the book of al-Tirmidhī on the Seal of Saints[250]

The saint of God is one who stands firm in his rank and lives up to the condition set by God, just as he lived up to sincerity in the journey to God, and to patience in acts of obedience and in performing the requirements of the religion. He practices the religious obligations and guards the legal limits. He holds to this station until he becomes steadfast, refined, cleansed, instructed, purified, scented, expanded, increased, promoted, and secured. Thus does God complete his sainthood by these ten qualities. Then he is taken from his place to the Sovereign Lord, and He grants him a rank between His hands. He comes to converse with God in intimacy. He becomes completely engaged with God to the exclusion of all else. Through God he is diverted from his ego-self and from everything else. God takes him in His grasp, and there is no protection stronger than His grasp, and no guardianship (for his mind) stronger than the divine intellect (ʿaql*ihi*).

And this was expressed by the following words of the Messenger of God, which he received from God through the Angel Gabriel: "Nothing causes My servant to draw near to Me as much as performing My religious obligations. But verily in addition to that he draws near to Me through supererogatory works, so that I come to love him. And when I have come to love him, I am his hearing, his sight, his tongue, his hand, his foot, his hand. Through Me he hears and through Me he sees, through Me he speaks and through Me he grasps, and through Me he walks and through Me he thinks and through Me he strikes." This servant's intellect has become extinguished in the Greatest Intellect, and his movements of passion have become still in the grasp of God.

---

250 The following passage is similar to that translated in Bernd Ratke and John O'Kane, *The Concept of Sainthood in Early Islamic Mysticism: Two works by Al-Hakim Al-Tirmidhi* (RoutledgeCurzon, 1996), 91-92. But there appear to be significant divergences between the text cited here than that translated by Ratdke and O'Kane. The translation here is therefore independent of that in *Concept of Sainthood*.

The Seal of Saints

Al-Ḥakīm al-Tirmidhī was asked, "What is the nature of this saint to whom belongs the Imamate, leadership, and Seal of sainthood?"

He replied, "He is close (in rank) to the Prophets, in fact he has nearly attained their status."

The student asked, "Then where is his station (*maqām*)?"

He replied, "His station is in the highest rank of the friends of God in the realm of singleness. Indeed, he stands isolated in God's Oneness. He converses intimately with God in the assemblies of the heavenly realms, and the gifts he receives are from the treasuries of exertion."

The student asked, "What are the treasuries of exertion?"

He replied, "There are three sorts of treasuries: the treasuries of favors for the saints of God, the treasuries of exertion for this leader and imam, and the treasuries of divine proximity for the Prophets, upon them peace."[251]

Shaykh Ibrāhīm Niasse, may God be pleased with him, indicated this station in one of his speeches, explaining that the Seal of Saints Shaykh Aḥmad al-Tijānī drank from the ocean of the Muḥammadan reality (*al-ḥaqīqa al-Muḥammadiyya*) along with the Prophets, on them peace. Thus do they drink both prophecy and sainthood. This is reflected in the Shaykh's statement, "As for the salt-water ocean, those who drink from it drink nothing but salt. The exceptions are the fish, which drink sweet water. This is due to their station from God, on account of His wisdom. Surely, if they were to drink salt water, they would (also) die."

The Identity of the Seal of the Saints

Here is the summary of what al-Tirmidhī had to say in his book concerning the Seal of the Saints. He was asked, "Can you describe for us this enraptured one to whom you found belonged the Imamate over all of the saints:

251 This preceding dialogue is contained in al-Tirmidhī's *Kitāb sīrat al-awliyā'*, see Radtke and O'Kane, *Concept of Sainthood*, 130-131.

the one in whose hand is the banner of sainthood; the one whose intercession is required by all of the saints, the same as the Prophets require that of our Prophet Muḥammad, God's blessing and peace upon him?"

He said, "As for his description, it is the same as I taught you."

He was asked, "By what has he gained precedence over the other saints, so that they need him?"

He said, "By his being given the Seal of Sainthood, and by this Seal he has gained precedence over them. Thus has he become the proof (*hujja*) of God against His saints."

And he mentioned in the beginning of the book that the reason for (the existence of) the Seal is as follows: "If Prophethood had been given to the Prophets, upon them peace, without their having been given the Seal, this bestowal would not have been free from the faults of the ego-self (*nafs*), so the *nafs* would have had its share in it. With our Prophet, prophecy was sealed, just as a contract is first written and then sealed so that no one can add to it or take away anything. I have thus described the Seal's affair for you.

"Similarly, God caused this Saint to progress along the way of Muḥammad, God's blessing and peace upon him. Just as Muḥammad, as God's Seal over prophecy, is the proof against the Prophets, so has this Saint become the proof against all the saints."[252]

Signs of the Saints

According to al-Ḥakīm al-Tirmidhī, the saints are those upon whom God the Most High has bestowed manifest celestial ranks. By this He has distinguished them with divine proximity, the light of majesty, the fear of arrogance, and the intimacy of reverence. Whoever looks upon the saint remembers God the Most High, testifying to the truth of the Prophet's statement: "The saints are the ones who invoke the remembrance of God when seen, for upon them can be witnessed the traces of the heavenly kingdom

---

252 A version of this section, with some divergences, can be found in Ratke and O'Kane, *Concept of Sainthood*, 186.

(*malakūt*)." Upon (the countenance of) such a saint is the light of God's sovereignty, grandeur and majesty. Your remembrance (when seeing the saint) is of God's grandeur, majesty, and sovereignty. Your astonishment in seeing him is due to God's light upon his heart, and God is the Light of lights.

As for the Seal of Saints, al-Ḥakīm al-Tirmidhī said: "There is among the saints a saint of the highest rank. God entrusted this servant for His work, and he is clenched firmly within His grasp. This servant turns by Him, speaks and hears by Him, sees by Him, strikes by Him, and thinks by Him. He is in His custody on the earth. God makes him the Imam of His creation, the bearer of the banner of the saints, the security for the denizens of the earth, the focal point for the denizens of the heavens, the perfume of the gardens. He is the elect of God, the subject of His gaze, the mine of His secret, and His voice on earth. By him, God guides His creation. In looking at him, the lifeless hearts are enlivened, and the creation is returned to His way. God's truths are refreshed by him. He is the key of guidance, and the lamp of the earth. He is the trustee of the list of saints and their leader. He upholds the praise of his Lord, in the presence of God's Messenger, God's peace and blessing upon him. The Messenger takes pride in him in this station, and God extols him with his (the Prophet's) name in this rank. He becomes the delight of the Messenger's eye. In summary, he is God's unique individual on the earth.

The Meaning of the Seal

According to Imam (ʿAbd al-Wahhāb) al-Shaʿrānī, as transmitted from (his) greatest of teachers, Sīdī Muḥammad Wafā:

> The first meaning of the "Seal" is the one who has obtained the utmost degree of axial sainthood (*quṭbaniyya*). He is the unique one, but in his time only, for the saintly pole (*quṭb*) is (also) the unique one of his age. In this way, there is no problem in saying that every age has a seal. The second meaning refers to him who is the Imām (al-Mahdī), whom God sends near the End of Time, who alone is entrusted with judgment and justice in that time, without doubt.

> The third meaning indicates the one by whom general esoteric sainthood is sealed, and he is also unique. And he is our master Jesus, upon him peace.
> As for the greatest of seals, which has sealed Muḥammadan sainthood, the meaning of this Seal is that there will not appear such perfection of (saintly) manifestation as appears with him alone, either before or after. And this is the meaning of the greatest seal, a Seal upon the heart of the Seal of Prophets.

This is what makes it incumbent to say that Shaykh al-Tijānī, may God be pleased with him, is the best of saints, for he is one of two (unique) saintly Seals (the other being Jesus). It was to this station of his that Shaykh Ibrāhīm Niasse pointed when he said in verse:

> The best of shaykhs of all time, without limit.
> Our Imam, the crown (*al-tijān*), endowed with the best of character.

This is the truth. Indeed, the Shaykh is one of the two saintly seals, and the two are the greatest inheritance. He, may God be pleased with him, is the seal of Muḥammadan sainthood, and our master Jesus, upon him peace, is the seal of unrestricted sainthood, insofar as he will descend (at the End of Time) to seal the (Muḥammadan) inheritance. The meaning of Shaykh Tijānī's being the Seal of Muḥammadan sainthood is that there will not appear one of this rank with such (saintly) manifestation as appears with him and in him. He is the Seal of perfected saintly manifestation.

Many of the greatest Imams, may God be pleased with them, mentioned this Seal. The first one we have found is the Imam of Ḥadīth and Sufism, Abū ʿAbdallāh Sīdī Muḥammad b. ʿAlī al-Tirmidhī "al-Ḥakīm", may God be pleased with him. The completeness of his spiritual experience was attested to by perfected gnostics, such as (Ibn ʿArabī) al-Ḥātimī and (Abū Ḥasan) al-Shādhilī.

As for Shaykh Muḥyī al-Dīn (Ibn ʿArabī), he mentioned this subject in a number of places in his book "The Meccan Illuminations" (*al-Futūḥāt al-makkiya*). He also composed a book specifically devoted to the subject, named "The Fabulous Gryphon concerning the Sun of Saints and the Seal of the Maghreb" (ʿUnqāʾ *mughrib fī shams al-awliyāʾ wa khatm al-maghrib*). Imam al-Shaʿrānī said that Muḥyī al-Dīn Ibn ʿArabī al-Ḥātimī once claimed this position for himself. He thought it belonged to him, just as a group among the truthful saints claimed this position. But this Greatest Shaykh reconsidered before death and came to know that this station did not belong to him, but to a saint afflicted by deniers. He mentioned that he saw him in Fez, and said, "his name is so and so, and his description is thus and such."

To make a long story short, the greatest Muḥammadan Seal is our Shaykh, our master, our teacher, our Imām, the perfected Shaykh, the comprehensive saintly pole, our patron Abū l-ʿAbbās (Aḥmad al-Tijānī), may God be pleased with him. And this (claim) is by way of firmly established confidence in his selection and what is due to him. He clearly related, in a manner that requires no further explanation, that the master of creation (the Prophet), God's blessing and peace upon him, informed him in a waking state that he was the well-known Seal of Muḥammadan sainthood over all the saintly poles and truthful saints. Indeed, there is no station (*maqām*) above his station in the matter of divine cognizance (*maʿrifa*). This Seal receives everything that flows from the presences of the Prophets, upon them blessing and peace, in terms of spiritual assistance (*amdād*). And he is the dispenser of this flood of assistance to entirety of saints, whether they know it or not. This is but one of the graces with which God distinguished him.

Among those who was instructed by our Shaykh, may God be pleased with him, was Sharīf Aḥmad al-Filālī, who recorded in his handwriting the dictation of our master, which I happened to find. To summarize, he concurred that one evidence that this station belonged to our Shaykh, may God be pleased with him, was that everyone (associated with him) held firmly to him until his passing, and not one of them differed in this matter. Then the matter became widely known among the elite and the generality of his companions and brethren in all the lands. (And Filālī wrote): "He did not turn away to disavow the one who disavowed him, whatever may have happened. He did not deny the one who denied him out of paucity of knowledge, restriction of the breast, or envy."

It has been demonstrated that the meaning of sealing in this station is that no other saint will appear with such manifest perfection as this Seal, may God be pleased with him, but it does not mean there will never be another saint after him.

Knowing Shaykh al-Tijānī, may God be pleased with him

In his book, "Priceless Rubies of the Distinguished Folk in the Maliki School" (*al-Yawāqīt al-thamīna fī aʿyān madhhab* ʿālim *al-madīna*), Muḥammad al-Bashīr Ẓāfir said in his biographical entry:

> Aḥmad b. Maḥammad b. al-Mukhtār b. Aḥmad b. Muḥammad b. Sālim al-Sharīf al-Tijānī: the renowned; the exemplar; the perfected; the cognizant of God; the one firmly rooted in the *Sunna* and the Religion; the profound, realized, and generous scholar; the one who combines the sacred law (*sharīʿa*) and the divine reality (*ḥaqīqa*), the rarity of the age, the lamp (*miṣbāḥ*) of the times.

Al-Kattānī said (in his biographical dictionary):

> He was, may God be pleased with him, one of the scholars who put his knowledge into action, one of the Imams of independent scholarly reasoning (*mujtahidīn*). He was among those who combined the honor of the source and the religion, the honor of knowledge, action, and certainty. He was endowed with lordly spiritual states and the highest of stations. His power was both manifest and unseen. He was the perfection of lights and excellences. He was dazzling to look at, and had a beautiful appearance, full of light in his elder years. He was possessed of a majestic awe, and magnanimous pardon. He was well known, and his fame spread far and wide. His state brought great benefit to others, and words had the habit of penetrating, commanding the good and forbidding the evil.

He was born in the year 1150/1737 in ʿAyn Māḍī. There he grew up in virtuousness and security, committed to earnestness and scholarly striving. He devoted himself to the Qurʾān, and then to learning the religious disciplines (ʿulūm), and the principles, the branches, and the manners pertaining to them. He mastered all of them and obtained their secret meanings. He learned the *Akhḍarī,* the *Muqaddama* of Ibn Rushd, the *Risālā*, and the *Mukhtaṣar* of Shaykh Khalīl[253] from Shaykh al-Mabrūk b. Abī ʿĀfiya al-Tijānī of ʿAyn Māḍī. He came to teach these subjects and to issue legal opinions. His mastery of the knowledge disciplines was clearly apparent. He revived and expanded upon both rational and transmitted knowledge, so he brought immense benefit.

Then he traveled to Fez in 1171/1758. There he studied Prophetic narrations (*ḥadīth*) and met Mawlay al-Ṭayyib al-Wazzāni and Mawlay Aḥmad al-Saqillī. Then he traveled to Tlemcen (Algeria). He stayed there to study Qurʾān exegesis (*tafsīr*) and *ḥadīth*, and other subjects besides. Then he performed the Pilgrimage in 1186/1772, passing by Tunis, and returning afterwards to Fez. Next, he traveled to Abū Samghūn,[254] where the Prophet, God's peace and blessing upon him, gave him license to instruct the creation. This was in the year 1196/1781. Then he left the desert and returned to Fez once again, coming to finally reside there in 1213/1798.

His virtues and spiritual states

He had many virtues and exalted spiritual states, may God be pleased with him. The scholars and imams of his time praised him on this account. Among them was the most eminent scholar Ḥamdūn b. al-Ḥājj,[255] who described him in verse as follows:

---

253 These are four formative texts consistent with an in-depth study of jurisprudence of the Mālikī school.

254 Abū Samghūn is an oasis settlement in southwest Algeria.

255 Ḥamdūn b. al-Ḥājj (d. 1817) was a famous Mālikī jurist of Fez and a contemporary to Shaykh al-Tijānī. He authored a famous commentary on Ibn ʿĀshir's *Murshid al-muʿīn*. As is apparent from the poem, Ibn al-Ḥājj eventually entered the Tijāniyya.

If you would like to enter early in gardens of security
And if you wish to nourish yourself in blessing and faith
Come to the full moon, the radiant light
Abū l-ʿAbbās Aḥmad al-Tijānī
The sun of spiritual mastery, the axis in the circle of guidance
Full moon of happiness, star of spiritual excellence
Ocean of generosity extending us wisdom and a path
Like the precious gems of the necklace and crown
The authoritative Imām, distinguished with ascensions
Possessed of righteous deeds, and he is never negligent.

Since the attainment of intimacy with the Messenger of God, peace and blessings upon him, Shaykh al-Tijānī underwent continuous training of the spirit. He attained an exalted rank and complete divine harmony, until he reached the station of the greatest axial sainthood (*al-quṭbāniyya al-*ʿuẓma). Then he arrived to the station of sainthood known among the saints as the Seal, and this was in the year 1214/1799, on a Monday, the 18th of Ṣafar, in the city of Fez. The author *Munyat al-murīd* (Aḥmad b. Bāba Shinqītī al-ʿAlawī) said:

In the month of Muḥarram, he became the rightly guided succor (*ghawth*)
The authority (*khalīfa*) of the Glorious Protector
And after a month, one night, he was elevated
To his mighty station, the ending point of all stations
His station is hidden from all others
Except the Prophet, and He who is behind him

After being established as the Hidden Pole (*al-quṭb al-maktūm*) and renowned isthmus (*al-barzakh al-maʿlūm*), Shaykh al-Tijāni said:

> The Hidden Pole is the intermediary between the Prophets, upon them peace and blessing, and the saints. The saints are unable to themselves receive the overflowing grace (*fayḍ*) from the Prophet, except after the Prophets have received it first. But he (the Hidden

> Pole) has a special mediation and support from the Prophet, for he receives directly from the Prophet without passing through the other Prophets. Indeed, he drinks from the presence of the Prophet Muḥammad, along with the Prophets.

I would like to conclude with a letter from Shaykh al-Tijānī that speaks about God's blessing on this Shaykh, the Seal of Saints:

> May the Peace, Mercy and Blessing of God be upon all of you. Writing to you is the servant in need of God, Aḥmad b. Maḥammad al-Tijānī. We ask God, mighty and majestic is He, that He protect you with His providential care, and that He flood you with the oceans of His bounty and friendship, and that He suffice you from any apprehension in this world and the next, that He save you from poverty in this world and punishment in the next.
>
> Know that God's bountiful grace (*faḍl*) has no limit, and that this bounty is in the Hand of God, who gives it to whom He wills.
>
> I say to you that our rank (*maqām*) with God in the next world has not been attained by any of the saints. They have not come close to it. Among all the saints from the time of the Prophet's Companions until the Day of Judgment, none has attained our rank or anything close to it. It is a desire beyond the reach of minds, unattainable for the greatest of the chivalrous (*fuḥūl*) because of the difficulty of the journey.
>
> I do not say this to you now except after hearing it confirmed by the Prophet Muḥammad, God's blessing and peace on him. There is not one of the distinguished folk (*al-rijāl*) whose companions will all enter Paradise without accounting or punishment, no matter the extent of their sins and disobedience, except I alone.
>
> Beyond what the Prophet, God's peace and blessing on him, has mentioned of this, he also guaranteed for my companions a matter that I am not permitted to mention. It cannot be seen or known until the next world.
>
> But with all of this, we do not jest about the sanctity (*ḥurma*) of our masters, the saints. We are not negligent in exalting them.

Therefore, exalt the sanctity of the saints, living and dead. Whoever exalts their sanctity, God exalts him. Whoever insults them, God humiliates him and is angry with him. We do not jest about the sanctity of the saints. Peace.

7.

What the Knowledgeable of God have said about the Knowledge of God

Address for the Birthday of Shaykh Ibrāhīm Niasse, Abidjan, Ivory Coast (2011)

In the Name of God, the Compassionate the Merciful

All praise belongs to God, who engendered fraternity between the souls before the appearance of bodies. We have learned from the words of the God's Prophet that the souls (*arwāḥ*) are like soldiers standing in rank. Those who knew each other before feel affinity in this realm and those who do not have differences. God the Most High said, "*And when your Lord took the children of Adam, from their loins, their descendants, and made them testify [saying to them], 'Am I not your Lord?' And they said, 'Yes indeed (balā)!'*"[256] So they responded with the letter *bā'*, out of which was what was, out of which is what is until the Day of Gathering.

May the prayer and peace of God be upon the secret of the Divine Essence (*dhāt*), the light of the Divine Essence, our Master Muḥammad, the light of existence (*wujūd*), the spiritual support (*madad*) of existence. There is no existence except his existence, no light except his light, no spiritual support except his support. And by this prayer may we come to the knowledge of him. The Lord of Might said, "I was an unknown treasure. Then I desired to be known, so I created the creation and made myself known to them. Then by Me (*fa-bī*) they know Me." And the letters of the word, "then by Me" (*fa-bī*) are equivalent to ninety-two, and these are also the numerological equivalent of the letters in the name "Muḥammad."[257] That is to say: it was by Muḥammad that the Exalted and Glorious Lord made Himself known. And may this prayer be on his pure family, his chosen Companions, and those who have succeeded them in spiritual excellence (*iḥsān*) till the Day of Judgment.

Distinguished leaders, ministers, princes, and directors; happy companions; distinguished imams, shaykhs, and instructors; his excellency, the noble, eminent master, the scholarly Sharīf 'Umar b. 'Abd

256 Qur'an, 7:172.

257 In Arabic numerology (*'ilm al-ḥurūf*), *fā'*=80, *bā'*=2, *yā'*=10; *mīm*=40, *ḥā'*=8, *dāl*=4; thus 80+2+10=92, and 40+8+40+4=92. For a reference chart concerning this system of numerology, see Annemarie Schimmel, *Mystical Dimensions of Islam* (Chapel Hill, UNC Press, 1975), xix-xx.

al-ʿAzīz,[258] who has taken responsibility for this blessed gathering, together with his noble brothers; to all you brothers and sisters gathered here from all corners of the earth in order to celebrate the birthday of our Master Shaykh Ibrāhīm Niasse: may God's peace, mercy, and blessing be upon you all.

God has facilitated my coming to this blessed place to meet with this large gathering of beloveds, among the citizens of the Ivory Coast and neighboring countries.[259] Our purpose is to discuss what is between us concerning the subject, "the knowledge of God" (*maʿrifa bi-Llāh*). The Sufi path, it is said, consists of both (individual) remembrance (*dhikr*) and collective reminding (*madhākara*). We hope that God Most High benefits us by what we hear, and allows us to hear what benefits us, in our final destination back to Him. He responds to those who raise their needs to Him. By Him do I speak, and my words are only by Him, from Him and to Him.

The Reality of the Knowledge of God

Imam Abū l-Qāsim ʿAbd al-Karīm b. Hūzān al-Qushayrī,[260] may God be pleased with him, described the knowledge of God as follows:

> Cognizance, gnosis, or awareness (*maʿrifa*)[261] is knowledge (ʿilm), for every knowing (ʿilm) is an awareness (*maʿrifa*), and every awareness is a knowing. Every knowledgeable person of God (ʿālim bi-Llāh) is a gnostic (*ʿārif*), and every gnostic is a scholar. In the terminology of

---

258 ʿUmar b. ʿAbd al-ʿAzīz, one of the prominent Tijānī *muqaddams* in the Ivory Coast, provided the live French translation of a version of this speech, the beginning of which can be found on Youtube: https://www.youtube.com/watch?v=56n0SUSFUxk (accessed 5 July 2022). As was often the case in delivering a live speech from prepared Arabic remarks, Shaykh al-Tijānī Cissé sometimes diverged from or reordered the text that he later presented to the translator of this volume.

259 The live speech mentioned in particular delegations from Ghana, Nigeria, Niger, and Gabon.

260 ʿAbd al-Karīm Abū l-Qāsim al-Qushayrī (d. 1072) was an early Sufi master from Khurasan.

261 The concept of *maʿrifa* is difficult to translate into English, which unlike Arabic (or French) does not distinguish between experiential knowledge (Arabic, *maʿrifa;* French, *connaissance*) and objectified knowledge (Arabic, *ʿilm;* French, *savoir*). This translation alternatively employs the English words cognizance, gnosis, or awareness to translate *maʿrifa.*

> the Sufis, gnosis (*maʿrifa*) is a description of those who know the Real, Glorious is He, by His Names and His Attributes, whom God has then confirmed in his affairs. Then God purifies him from his lowly traits and awakens him. Long he waits at the door in God's attendance, his heart persisting in worldly withdrawal, until God the Most High grants him the beauty of acceptance in His presence. God then confirms him in all of his words and cuts off from him the stray thoughts of his lower self (*nafs*). Nothing occurs to his heart that would invite him to other than God. Thus does he become a stranger to the creation, absolved from the heedlessness of his self, and purified from its fixations and petty observations. He secretly persists in his intimate discourse with God the Exalted. He ascertains the reality of every moment as having its return to God. The Real, Glorious is He, informs him (of each moment) beforehand, through an awareness that pervades him of the secrets of God's dispositions and capacities. It is at this point that he is named "gnostic" (ʿārif), and his spiritual state is called "gnosis" (*maʿrifa*). The gist of the matter is that a person obtains gnosis by his Lord to the extent of his alienation from his self.[262]

The Prophet David (Dāwūd), upon him be peace, once asked, "O Lord! How do I arrive to You?" The Lord, exalted is His majesty, said, "Leave your self, and come."

The hidden pole, our Master Aḥmad al-Tijānī, may God be pleased with him, was asked about the reality of knowing God Most High. He responded saying:

> True gnosis is when God takes a servant in such an embrace that he does not know origin (*aṣl*), differentiation (*faṣl*), or means (*sabab*). He does not discern a specified wherewithal, and nothing remains of his sensory feeling, individual witnessing, personal erasure, movement, or volition. What has befallen him by divine manifestation (*tajalla*) has no beginning and no end; it is not bound by delimitation or ending.

---

262 Abū l-Qāsim al-Qushayrī, *Risālat al-Qushayrīya*; see Qushayri's "Treatise on Sufism" in John Renard, *Knowledge of God in Classical Sufism* (New York: Paulist Press, 2004), 286-293. The translation here is independent of Renard's.

In the *Jawāhir al-maʿānī,* he also said, "The people of gnosis have passed away in God from everything that perishes. They see by the Majesty and Beauty of God, and they know by His Attributes and Names.

The pole of gnostics, the bringer of the Tijānī flood, our Master Shaykh Ibrāhīm Niasse, said:

> Gnosis is the rooting and establishment of the spirit (*rūḥ*) in the presence of witnessing, with complete annihilation and persistence by God. The gnostic among the Sufi people is the one who sees the Source (*ʿayn*) in otherness, meaning the one who witnesses the Real in otherness. For me, the gnostic is he who becomes annihilated in God's Essential Being (*dhāt*) once, then becomes annihilated in God's Attribute (*ṣifa*) twice or three times, and then becomes annihilated in the Name once. He attests to Being (*al-wujūd*) by the three Realities (*ḥaqāʾiq*), and he attests to the Names by the Name. This is a spiritual station obscured by thorns and the shredding of livers. It cannot be obtained by the giving of money or (having lots of) children. The master of this station is possessed of perfect wakefulness. He is perfectly content with God, with His wisdom, with His rulings, and with the entirety of His decrees. And God is pleased with him, and he becomes deserving of His words, "*So enter among my righteous servants, and enter My Paradise.*"[263]

He also said, may God be pleased with him: "Gnosis means the unveiling (*kashf*) of God's Names and Attributes, resulting in the observance (*murāqaba*) of God and the sincerity of action for His sake." And he said, "The reality of gnosis is the witnessing of the perfection of God's Essential Being: '*And there is nothing the like comparable to Him.*'"[264] And he also said, "The one acquainted with God does not derive pleasure from anything else in the creation, and the one acquainted with the lower world (*dunyā*) has no pleasure in his life. Who has his insight opened is astonished and made silent: he does not occupy himself with words."

---

263 The Qur'ān verse mentioned is 89:29-30.

264 The Qur'ān verse referenced is 42:11.

The Greatest Shaykh Muḥyī al-Dīn Ibn ʿArabī[265] said: "Know that gnosis is of two types: general gnosis, and special gnosis. As for the first, this is the gnosis obtained by seeking evidence, and it is called 'certain knowledge' (ʿilm al-yaqīn). As for the second, it has two types: the 'eye of certainty' (ʿayn al-yaqīn) and knowledge of the 'absolute truth' (*ḥaqq al-yaqīn*). The first is obtained by means of the witnessed (creation), and it is the station of the elite saints. The second is gnosis the spirit obtains by the eye of the witnessing (*ʿayn al-mushāhada*). This is when the senses of the heart become tranquil of the self's turbidities, freed from the chains of carnality, and purified from base human characteristics. At this point the knowledge of God the Exalted becomes manifest to the spirit."

(Abū Bakr) al-Shiblī[266] said, "The gnostic does not look to other than Him. He does not speak words by other than Him. He does not see any guardian for himself other than God the Exalted."

Some of the Sufi people have said, "Gnosis is when the Real causes you to die to your self and brings you to life by Him." And it is said, "The gnostic becomes intimate with the remembrance of God and flees from the creation. He presents his needs to God, and God makes him independent of His creation. He humbles himself before the Most High, and then God exalts him among His creation."

Abū l-Ṭayyib al-Sāmirī[267] said: "Gnosis is the Real's sunrise upon (a person's) secret, innermost being through the arrival of lights." And it has been said, "The gnostic is more than what is said, the scholar is less than what is said."

---

265 Widely known as the "greatest shaykh" within the Sufi tradition, Ibn ʿArabī (d. 1230, Damascus) was originally from Andalusia. He formulized a good deal of the later terminology of the Sufi tradition. Among other sources on Ibn ʿArabī, see William Chittick, *The Sufi Path of Knowledge: Ibn al-ʿArabī's Metaphysics of Imagination* (Albany: SUNY Press, 1989).

266 Abū Bakr al-Shiblī (d. 946, Baghdad) was an important early Sufi and disciple of Imam Junayd.

267 The translator has been unable to identify this scholar, but the name appears with this citation in al-Qushayrī's *Risāla fī ʿilm al-taṣawwuf.* Elsewhere in the *Risāla,* al-Sāmirī is referenced as relating knowledge from al-Junayd al-Baghdādī, thus presumably his student. See Knysh, *al-Qushayri's Epistle*, 137, 323. Al-Sulamī (d. 1021, Neyshabur) alternatively ascribes the same attributed quote to al-Junayd al-Baghdādī. See Abū ʿAbd al-Raḥmān Muḥammad al-Sulamī, *al-Muqaddima fī l-taṣawwuf* (Beirut: Dar al-Kutub, 1971), 16.

Al-Junayd[268] said, "The gnostic is he to whom God has enunciated His secret, and he has kept quiet."[269]

(Abū) Yaʿqūb al-Sūsī[270] was asked, "Does the gnostic feel grief on account of anything other than God the Mighty and Majestic?" He said, "Does he see anything besides him on whose account to be grieved?" Then he was asked, "By what eye does he look at things?" He said, "With the eye of annihilation (in God) and perishing (of the world)."

It has been said, "The gnostic is the one whose eye cries, but whose heart laughs."

Al-Junayd said, "The gnostic is not knowledgeable until he is like the earth, enclosing both righteousness and corruption, or like the cloud shading everything, or like the rain quenching the thirst of those it loves and those it does not love."

Abū Yazīd (al-Bistāmī)[271] said, "They have obtained gnosis by forsaking what belongs to them, and by stopping with what belongs to Him."

Ibn ʿAṭāʾ-Allāh[272] said, "Gnosis is based on three pillars: fear (*hayba*), modesty (*ḥayā*ʾ), and intimacy with God (*uns*)."

It was said to Dhū l-Nūn al-Miṣrī,[273] "How did you come to know your Lord?" He said, "I came to know my Lord by my Lord, and if not for my Lord, I would not have known my Lord."

It has been said, "The scholar is emulated, but the gnostic is followed."

One of the shaykhs was asked, "How did you come to know God the Exalted?" He said, "By a light shining forth from the tongue, taken from

---

268 Al-Junayd al-Baghdādī (d. 910), often called "The Imam of this (Sufi) collective", was one of the most preeminent early Sufis within the Abbasid Caliphate centered in Baghdad. See Ali Abdel-Kader, *The Life, Personality and Writings of al-Junayd: a Study of a Third/Ninth Century Mystic with an edition and translation of his writings* (London: Luzac, 1976).

269 An alternative translation of this statement could be, "The Real speaks from the innermost being (*sirr*) of the gnostic, while he remains silent." Knysh's version from al-Qushayrī's *Risāla* reads, "The gnostic is someone on behalf of whose innermost soul God speaks, while he remains silent" (*Epistle*, 323).

270 Little is known about this early Sufi, except that he was also cited as an authority on the ways of early Sufism in al-Qushayrī's *Risāla*. See Knysh, *al-Qushayri's Epistle*, 322.

271 Abū Yazīd al-Bistāmī (d. 874) was an early Persian Sufi known by later Sufis as "The Sultan of Gnostics." He was renowned for his ecstatic utterances.

272 Ibn ʿAṭā-Allāh al-Iskandarī (d. 1309, Cairo) was a prominent scholar and Sufi of the Shādhiliyya Sufi order in Egypt.

273 Dhū l-Nūn Thawbān al-Miṣrī (d. 859, Cairo) was an early Egyptian Sufi famous for his reflections on gnosis (*maʿrifa*), and thought to have been the shaykh of Sahl al-Tustari (d. 896).

the differentiated one contracted (with God's secret), and from the expression passing from the tongue of an annihilated, lost one; pointing towards the finding of a (divine) manifestation, preferring the secret above all else. This is how it came to be." And there are many other expressions of this sort. As the poet has said:

I uttered without utterance; He is the utterance
For You is the pronouncing of the utterance, or to explain out of the utterance
You appeared where before You had been hidden
A flash of lightning burst upon me, and I burst forth with lightning.

It has been said of the gnostic's description: "Nothing makes him impure, and everything is purified by him."

Dhū l-Nūn al-Miṣrī said, "The signs of the gnostic are three: the light of his gnosis does not block out the light of his pious restraint (*wara'*); he does not believe that inner, esoteric knowledge ('ilm al-bāṭin) abolishes the need to follow outward legal injunctions; and the many gifts and blessings given to him by God does not incite him to rend the veils that cover God's hidden sanctity."

Abū Sa'īd al-Kharrāz (al-Baghdādī)[274] said, "Gnosis comes from an eye that weeps abundantly, and from expending the utmost effort."

Al-Junayd was asked about the saying of Dhū l-Nūn al-Miṣrī describing the gnostic, "He was here but now he has gone." Junayd replied, "One spiritual state does not hold the gnostic back from another spiritual state, and one spiritual station does not veil him from changing stations. Thus is he with the people of every place just as they are: he experiences whatever they experience, and he speaks their language so that they might benefit by his speech."

Muḥammad b. al-Faḍl[275] said, "Gnosis is the life of the heart with God."

---

274 Abū Sa'īd al-Kharrāz (d. 899) of Baghdad was an early Sufi associated with the concept of "annihilation" (*fanā'*) in God.

275 Muḥammad b. Ibrāhīm b. al-Faḍl was an early Sufi from whom al-Qusharyī took narrations in his *Risāla*. See Knysh, *al-Qushayri's Epistle*, 325.

Ibn as-Sammāk was asked, "When does the servant know that he has attained the reality of gnosis?" He answered, "When the servant comes to witness the Real with the eye of esteem and respect, and when he passes away from everything other than Him."

Yaḥyā b. Muʿādh,[276] may God have mercy on him, said, "Gnosis is the proximity of the heart to the Ever Near (*al-Qarīb*), the spirit's vigilant awareness of the Beloved (*al-Ḥabīb*), and the isolation of oneself from everything else with the Sovereign responsive to prayers (*al-Mālik al-mujīb*)."

It has been narrated that God the Exalted once revealed to the Prophet Dāwūd, peace be upon him, "O Dāwūd! Come to know Me and come to know yourself!" So Dāwūd meditated on these words and said, "My God! I have come to know You through Your transcendental uniqueness (*fardaniyya*), might (*qudra*) and everlasting permanence (*baqāʾ*); and I have come to know myself through my incapacity (*ʿajz*) and annihilation (*fanāʾ*)."

I would add here that the knowledge of God, glorious and exalted is He, is, according to these meanings, the utmost goal and aspiration of the ascetics and the highest degree hoped to be attained by the reverent folk. Thus, the Sufi people have been thrust on to the path of obtaining this most precious and invaluable acquisition. They have spent their lives in its pursuit, leaving their homelands on its account, undergoing extreme difficulties and passing through severe ordeals until they achieved victory in its attainment. Some of them have turned back empty handed from failing to fulfill its prerequisites or patiently endure its weighty affair without realizing anything of its reality. It is enough for you as an example to recall the story of Prophet Moses (Mūsā) and his companion, Khiḍr, peace be upon them both. Mūsā was among the arch-Prophets, but he could not bear patiently with the testing and examination of Khiḍr. Thus did he have to return without obtaining anything of this Divine Knowledge (ʿilm al-ladunī), although he went on the journey with the express intention of acquiring such knowledge.

For this reason has such knowledge been referred to as "the rarest treasure" and the one in possession of it has been referred to as "the

276 Yaḥyā b. Muʿādh al-Rāzī (d. 871) was another early Sufi from whom al-Qusharyī took narrations in his *Risāla*. See Knysh, *al-Qushayri's Epistle*, 329.

philosophers stone" or "the red sulphur" (*al-kibrīt al-aḥmar*). However, since the appearance of the Saintly Seal (Shaykh Aḥmad al-Tijānī), the distance to its arrival has been folded up and made short. The knowledge has been spread among the people of his spiritual path and circulated among his followers, and with the manifestation of the bringer of the Tijani flood—our Master Shaykh Ibrāhīm b. al-Ḥājj ʿAbdallāh Niasse—there has been an effusion of Divine knowledge and gnosis. Everyone has drunk from its contents, until the knowledge of God has spread to practically every land. All who have a connection with this honorable saintly pole (*quṭb*) have been blessed with their share, and no one has been given a greater portion than them in this day and age. Such people are scholars, leaders, imams and princes. They are stars and lamps of guidance in every land.

The Path to Gnosis

The bringer of the Tijani spiritual flood, our master Shaykh Ibrāhīm Niasse quoted (in his book *Kāshif al-ilbās*) the distinguished scholar and knower of God, Sidi Muḥammad al-Yadālī[277] from his *Sharḥ khātimat al-ṭaṣawwuf*:

> It has been said that the quickest way to enter the Divine Presence is through the remembrance of God (*dhikr*), because the Name is inseparable from the One named. Since the one engaged in remembrance ceaselessly mentions the Name of God, the veils are torn to shreds bit by bit, until the heart comes to witness God directly. When this happens, the spiritual aspirant dispenses with the remembrance due to his witnessing the One remembered. This is what the Sufi people mean by entering the Divine Presence of God: the removal of veils so that you enter the Divine Presence while you remain sitting in your place.

277 Muḥammad al-Yadālī (d. 1753) was a prominent scholar of the Shādhiliyya Sufi order in what is today the state of Mauritania.

Al-Yadālī also said in *Sharh shahiyyat al-samāʿ*:

> A servant does not draw near to His Exalted Presence unless he displays a deep sense of modesty and bashfulness. He does not perfect this (disposition) unless he obtains spiritual illumination (*kashf*) and the lifting of the veils; and he does not perfect this (*kashf*) unless he perseveres in the remembrance. Constant engagement in the remembrance is the only way to perfect the station of complete sincerity, where one sees all actions as the creation of God. There is no other way to cut off the evil, satanic thoughts, nor are the egocentric delusions weakened by any other means. The continued practice of the remembrance causes the anxiety and sadness of the world to disappear, for such emotions are only a result of the heedlessness of God. Indeed, the servant has no one to blame but himself if anxieties and sorrows should afflict him in unrelenting succession, for these are only the consequence of turning away from his Lord. He who desires persistent happiness must devote himself to persistent remembrance.
>
> Some of the deluded and misguided folk have become stagnant, contenting themselves with the gatherings of remembrance (*majlis al-dhikr*) in the morning and evening, while remaining heedless of God in between. But this practice is of no use for the spiritual wayfarer (*sālik*) who seeks the station of the Sufi people. Perhaps he who contends with this will cite the prophetic saying: "If the servant remembers his Lord for a time at the beginning and end of the day, he will be forgiven whatever comes between." However, forgiveness does not include spiritual advancement (*tarqiya*). The object of seeking forgiveness is to equate a person with one who has not sinned, not to associate him with the one who has performed acts of worshipful obedience. Understand that the desire of the Sufi people is continuous spiritual elevation with each breath, through the remembrance of God, so that they do not regard themselves as having fulfilled one atom of God's right on them.

Gnosis with the Sufi people is the acquisition of the knowledge of God as it relates to His Essential Being, Attributes, Names and Actions. This is the most important of the religious obligations and the most sublime honor, as it is the foundation of the faith and the goal of Islam. The gnosis of God is the utmost goal in the perfection of the human condition, the highest rank of spiritual realization, and the most cherished ideal. None obtains the rank of Divine gnosis except that he has been permitted through all of the waystations of the spiritual journey, and that with firm step, strong faith, and sound heart. The knowledgeable one of God does not have knowledge until he folds up the waystations of the path to God. Humankind's knowledge of God is above all other types of knowledge.

None is given the strength to attain this degree unless he has begun his journey with correct comportment (*adab*), for the rectitude of his external and internal states depends on the proper comportment. He then obtains what is desired in both his deeds and words, without discomfort or effort. His attributes are perfected, a completion of the light of Divine Perfection. Such a person is elevated from perfection to a greater perfection. From proper comportment, his character acquires light. He is illumined with guidance, and the Real causes him to shed light. His spirit is nurtured with the rubies of realities. He consecrates himself to God, with utter sincerity in the religion for His sake. His heart blooms with faith, and his intention is purified externally and internally.

Who knows God with the knowledge that befits Him walks among the creation as the semblance of the excellences of the most exalted attributes. He is of the best comportment in his words, actions, and spiritual state. He desires good for his brother in faith, the same as he desires for himself. He directs himself to God with a pure heart, mature belief, firm faith, feet firmly planted, and with elevated spiritual experience. His goal is God. The Shaykh of Islam, our master Shaykh Ibrāhīm Niasse said:

> The quickest way to achieve gnosis is by following the Messenger of God, may the peace and blessings of God be upon him, in his statements, actions, spiritual states, and character, and in honoring the rights of God publicly and privately. He has absolute sincerity with God the Exalted, without any worldly or otherworldly motive. He is like this only for the sake of God the Exalted, glorifying and exalting

> Him. He does this with open pleasure, submission, trust, and dependence on God the Exalted in every single thing.

The consummate scholar, Sīdī Muḥammad b. al-Mashrī al-Sabāʿī al-Sāʾihī,[278] related a narration concerning the Hidden Pole Sīdī Aḥmad al-Tijānī in the book, *Rawḍ al-muḥibb al-fānī*:

> As for the true reality of the Shaykh of Arrival (*shaykh al-wāṣil*), he is the one for whom all of the veils have been removed from the perfect beholding of the Divine Presence, with visual perception and certain realization. The process begins with attentive awareness (*muḥāḍara*), which entails observing the realities from behind a thick curtain. Next comes disclosure (*mukāshifa*), which entails observing the realities from behind a thin curtain. Then comes direct witnessing (*mushāhada*), which entails the manifestation of the realities without a veil (*hijāb*), but with particularity. Last comes the direct beatific vision, which entails observing the realities without veil or particularity, with absolutely no surviving trace of otherness. This is the station of eradication, destruction, annihilation, and the annihilation of annihilation.
>
> There is nothing in this station except the direct vision of the Real, in the Real, for the Real, and by the Real.
>
> Nothing remains except God, and nothing besides Him.
>
> There is nothing to be added and nothing to be separated.
>
> Then comes the real life and true existence, in which one is able to distinguish the degrees on the basis of direct experiential knowledge (*maʿrifa*) of their particularities, requirements, exigencies and everything to which they are entitled. One will know, as well, the source for each degree, the reason for its existence, its intended purpose, and the return of its affairs. This is the station of the servant's comprehension of his personal identity and his knowledge of all its secrets and particularities; as well as his knowledge of the Divine

---

278 Muḥammad b. al-Mashrī (or al-Mishrī, d. 1809, Algeria) was one of the earliest companions of Shaykh Aḥmad al-Tijānī, known for his proximity to the Shaykh, his expertise in Islamic learning, and for composing a number of important works. See Wright, *Realizing Islam*, 12-13.

Presence, Its grandeur, majesty, exalted attributes and perfection. And this knowledge of his will be the product of direct experience and indubitable vision.

Vast deserts must be traversed for the holder of such a degree. In spite of hardships, the effort is perfectly worthwhile, since the Real has granted him a specific authorization (*idhn*) to provide right guidance to His servants and has charged him with the task of directing them towards the Divine Presence.

The Doctrine of Unity among the Gnostics

The consummate scholar Sīdī Muḥammad b. al-Mashrī (also) reported in *Rawḍ al-muḥibb al-fānī*:

> Shaykh Aḥmad al-Tijānī was asked about the doctrine of unity among the gnostic sages (*tawḥīd al-ʿārifīn*), and its difference with the doctrine of unity (*tawḥīd*) among the speculative theologians (*mutakallimīn*). He responded, may God be pleased with him, by saying:
> "As for the *tawḥīd* of the speculative theologians, they have offered a sort of remedy for the health of *tawḥīd*, demonstrating what constitutes incapacity, imperfection or ignorance in the description of the Creator, glorious and exalted is He. They have offered all of this with rational proofs based on what has been firmly established. However, these theologians find themselves in great difficulty from the plethora of successive analogies. This type of *tawḥīd* should not preoccupy a person, due to the abundance of doubt and confusion therein.
> "As for the *tawḥīd* of the gnostics, this is the worship of One God, with contentment and submission to the judgment of One God. In all of their conditions, they depend only on the One God. They direct their aspirations and their hearts only to the One God. They have no longing except for One God. Their goal in the beginning, middle and end of their journey is only for the One God.
> "All of this is through the dismissal of passion (*hawa*) externally and internally, in both essence and trace. The servant is at the remotest

distance from the draping of the ego-self (*nafs*), passion, and Satan. If there should occur to him the slightest inclination towards passion, even the smallest grain or speck of dust, he may not ascribe oneness to the One God. He cannot be described as having worshipped One God. When they have this sort of (pure) *tawḥīd*, they build for it a fortress and become established in it. They become drowned in the ocean of Divine satisfaction and submission, knowing from Him that nothing escapes the rule (*ḥukm*) of the One God, the sweetness and the bitterness, the good and the bad. No one has any choice along with Him, for if there were a choice other than His, there would be a god beside Him.

"Who has correctly implemented the aforementioned descriptions is at ease with whatever affliction. He sits on the carpet of tranquility and comfort, with a robe of honor that melts away the difficulty, the misfortune of self-direction, in which he was previously engaged. There he sits with God on the carpet of proximity and intimacy. He does not beg for what he finds of provision, gifts, wealth, the fulfillment of all desires. This is from God's might, majesty, and bestowal of honor, for which there is no limit or enumeration.

"This is the *tawḥīd* of the gnostics referred to by the saintly pole Mawlay ʿAbd al-ʿAzīz al-Dabbāgh,[279] may God be pleased with him. He said it was being free from the difficulty of defending analogies successively piled up by the theologians. The *tawḥīd* of the gnostics does not cling to analogies."

Then Shaykh al-Tijānī, may God be pleased with him, said, "The likeness of this is as two people. One of them is deeply afflicted by sickness. As soon as one sickness leaves him, one greater comes to take its place. He devotes his attention to searching for cures, to knowing the sickness, its sources, causes, and remedy. But how can he obtain such (a complete cure), given his defective state, limited time, isolation, and constitution? For he finds himself in great difficulty comprehending these sciences, and every time he makes

---

279 ʿAbd al-ʿAzīz al-Dabbāgh (d. 1719, Fez) was an important seventeenth-century Moroccan Sufi known as the saintly pole (*quṭb*) of his time, some of whose later descendants became disciples of Shaykh Aḥmad al-Tijānī.

a mistake in anything, harm afflicts him. He wastes most of his journey occupied with these sciences.

"As for the other person, he comes forth in perfect health and strength. God secures him from pestilence and affliction. No sickness befalls him. Since he does not himself experience any sickness, he is unaware of the knowledge of medicine, and of all of its exigencies and aggravating circumstances.

"So the first one says to the other one, 'Your ignorance of medicine is the source of great harm!' But the other one says to the first, 'Only those like you, infected with sickness, require medicine. As for me, I am not sick, so I have no need of medicine.'"

Then he was asked, "Why has this *tawḥīd* (of the gnostics) not appeared in books and poetry collections to provide benefit to everyone?"

He said, "The answer is that the gnostics have not hidden it, for this *tawḥīd* was that sent with all of the Messengers, and it was this which was manifested to the generality of the creation. But the theologians left this and studied a way to deny this (original) *tawḥīd* from the general population. This was for the purpose of inclining them to the useless saddlebags of theology, its rules and methodology, by means of rational proofs and demonstrations. Among them there were those who thought that this was the height of proximity to God the Exalted and the perfection of knowledge. But they did not know that this was misguidance, and that it placed them in the farthest distance from God.

"The reason that the common folk fell into the confusion of the theologians was the discovery of the earlier sciences of (Hellenist) philosophy. Philosophy became established in their knowledge as the 'science of *tawḥīd*.' The truth is that the search for Divine knowledge through rational laws and logical demonstrations is the means by which God removed them from the knowledge of the Truth, from approaching with that which draws near to God, and from the awareness of His Majesty.

"When this third knowledge of philosophy entered the hearts, and they heard this as the discipline of *tawḥīd*, these saddlebags, articulated now in Arabic, changed them from the people of Divine favor to

> those who rejected God the Exalted. Generally, all who obtained this science leaped into ignorance, while claiming that they had reached the pinnacle of knowledge. But they were far removed from the knowledge of God and the awareness of His Majesty.
>
> "They expounded to the common folk that whoever did not know their science was as if he knew nothing. The souls of the common folk followed them, inclined towards worldly favor, for they saw how they were exalted in the hearts of the commoners, kings, and princes. On account of following this whirlwind, which differed from the righteous forefathers (*salaf*) without any excuse or restraint, the true knowledge of *tawḥīd* sent with the Messengers was forgotten. Those who sought the *tawḥīd* of the Messengers came to reject the *tawḥīd* of the philosophers as poison for the Sufis and gnostics. And indeed, those who sought the *tawḥīd* of the philosophers became as poison for theology itself.
>
> "As for the interjection into the discipline of theology by gnostics such as al-Ashʿarī and al-Sanūsī and their like, may God be pleased with them, it was only their desire for kindness with the common folk. When it was (argued) that (disputes over) the *tawḥīd* of the Messengers cannot be answered except by the sword, they answered that the commoners could accept the command of God by their own volition if they were given foundational rational proofs (for the correct *tawḥīd*). They saw that this was better than the sword, for the one forced by the sword does not enter the religion except under compulsion and force. This was the reason for their interjection into the science of theology." As for the "Unity of Existence" (*waḥdat al-wujūd*), his words on that subject will be presented later on.

Imam (Abū Ḥāmid) al-Ghazālī, may God have mercy on him, divided *tawḥīd* into four degrees in his *Iḥyā ʿulūm al-dīn*: the core, the core of the core, the shell, and the shell of the shell. He said:

> The first degree of *tawḥīd* is when a person says with his tongue, "There is no god but God." But his heart is heedless of the statement, or even in denial of it, as with the *tawḥīd* of the hypocrites. The second

degree is when the heart testifies to the meaning of the enunciation, as the generality of the Muslim so testify. This is the belief of the common people. The third is when a person witnesses this (belief) by way of spiritual unveiling (*kashf*) through the light of the Real. This is the station of those drawn near, for they see many things, but despite their multiplicity, they see them as having originated from the One, the Compeller. The fourth degree is when a person does not see anything in existence except the One. This is the witnessing of the most truthful ones (*ṣiddīqīn*). The Sufis call this the annihilation (*fanāʾ*) in *tawḥīd*. This is because when such a person sees nothing but the One, he does not see himself. As he does not see himself due to his complete absorption in *tawḥīd*, (it is correct to say) he has passed away from himself in *tawḥīd*. The meaning here is that he has passed away from seeing himself, and from seeing the entirety of creation.

Muḥammad b. Mūsā al-Wāsiṭī[280] said, "All forms of *tawḥīd* that are articulated by tongues, pointed out by explanation and (thus) subject to exaggeration, abstraction, or separation (*tafrīd*), are infected with sickness. The reality is other than that."

Our Master and our Shaykh Aḥmad al-Tijānī, may God be pleased with him, said: "As long as you see that you exist and that God exists, so that there are two, where is the Oneness (*tawḥīd*)? Oneness only exists if the Oneness is by God, from God, and to God. The servant does not enter into it nor exit from it. And this is not realized except by way of annihilation (*fanāʾ*)."

If it were established that the Real were separate from the existence (*wujūd*), He would be absent (*mafqūd*), and beyond your aspiration. Ibn ʿAjība explained the words in the *Ḥikam* (of Ibn ʿAṭāʾ-Allāh), "Let not the goal of your aspiration be shifted to other than Him, for one's hopes cannot exceed the Generous Lord (*al-Karīm*)." He said, "O aspirant! Attach your aspiration to God for what you want, not to anything else besides Him. He is always Generous, and His blessing flows night and day. The Generous Lord is not exceeded by hopes, and He loves to be asked so that He may answer."

---

280 Abū Bakr Muḥammad b. Mūsā al-Wāsiṭī (d. 932, Merv), originally from Khurasan, was among the authorities of early Sufism relied upon by al-Qushayrī. See Knysh, *al-Qushayrī's Epistle*, 58.

The Need for Companionship with a Gnostic Sage

Know that the aspirant does not benefit from the knowledge and spiritual states of the shaykh unless he submits to him with complete obedience, believing in his excellence and (spiritual) completion. He must stop where the shaykh orders him to stop. It is not for the disciple to (simply) enrich the shaykh, as is the practice of some people. They believe in the shaykh's utmost perfection and think that this will suffice them in obtaining the goal. But they do not follow his example, nor carry out what he commands them to do, nor hold back from what he has forbidden them. What follows here are some of the statements of the gnostics concerning the need (*ḍarūra*) for (Sufi) companionship and its benefits.

Ibn ʿAjība[281] said in the Īqāẓ al-himam: "The shaykh of shaykhs Sīdī ʿAlī al-Jamal, may God be pleased with him, said in his book that the best way for the student to approach God the Exalted is by sitting with the knowledgeable one (ʿārif) of God if he can find him. Sitting with the gnostic is better than seclusion (ʿuzla); and seclusion is better than sitting with the heedless common folk; and sitting with the heedless is better than sitting with the ignorant disciple (*al-faqīr al-jāhil*). This is because the gnostic brings the aspirant to his Lord with a glance or with a word, while the ignorant disciple cuts him off from his Lord with a glance or a word. There is nothing better than sitting with the gnostic."

The story of Prophet Moses (Mūsā), upon him peace, and Khiḍr is strong evidence on the need for companionship with a gnostic shaykh, the submission to him and the obedience to his command in order obtain what is desired, Divine gnosis. The gnostic Amīr ʿAbd al-Qādir al-Jazā'irī[282] said in his book *al-Mawāqif*:

> Moses, upon him peace, whatever the greatness of his own capacity and the exaltedness of his affair, sought out the meeting with

---

281 Aḥmad b. ʿAjība (d. 1809, Tetuan) was an influential scholar and writer associated with the Darqawiyya branch of the Shādhiliyya Sufi order.

282 ʿAbd al-Qādir al-Jazā'irī (d. 1883, Damascus) led the Algerian resistance against French occupation in the mid-nineteenth century, and later came to reside in Syria where he gained renown as a prominent scholar and Sufi associated with the Qādiriyya order.

Khiḍr, upon him peace. He suffered aching longing and difficulty in his journey, as he said, *"Surely we have suffered much fatigue at this stage in our journey."*[283] With all of this, he was unable to bear with one interdiction, which was Khiḍr's saying, *"Do not ask me any questions until I speak to you about it."*[284] So Moses did not benefit from the knowledge of Khiḍr, even though Moses was absolutely certain that Khiḍr, as confirmed by God the Exalted, had more knowledge than him. When Moses said, "I do not know anyone more knowledgeable than I am," God said, "Nay, with us is Khiḍr." As Moses did not specify one type of knowledge over another, his statement was a generalization.

Moses in the beginning was not aware that he was unprepared to accept anything from the knowledge of Khiḍr. But Khiḍr knew this right away, so he said, *"You will not be able to have patience with me."*[285] Khiḍr, upon him peace, knew this from knowledgeable insight. Let the intelligent contemplate the exemplary conduct (*adab*) of these two masters.

Moses, upon him peace, asked, *"May I follow you so that you may teach me of what you have learned?"*[286] In other words, "Can you give me permission to follow you, in order to learn from you?" Such words reflect the sweetness of exemplary conduct that those of sound spiritual experience have tasted.

Khiḍr, upon him peace, said, *"If you should follow me, do not ask me any questions until I speak to you about it."*[287] He did not say, "Do not ask me anything!" and then remain silent so that Moses would have remained confused and languishing. Rather he promised to speak to him about it, to explain the wisdom of what he did.

283 Qur'ān, 18:62.

284 Qur'ān, 18:70.

285 Qur'ān, 18:67.

286 Qur'ān, 18:66.

287 Qur'ān, 18:70.

Ibn ʿAṭāʾ-Allāh Iskandarī, may God be pleased with him, said in *Miftāḥ al-falāḥ*:

> It is necessary for the one resolved on seeking guidance that he should follow the path of guidance, that he search out a shaykh among the folk of spiritual realization (*taḥqīq*). The one who walks this path leaves aside his passion. He plants his feet firmly in the service (*khidma*) of his master. When he finds him, he should implement what he commands and avoid what he forbids.

Ibn ʿAṭāʾ-Allāh also said in *Laṭāʾif al-minan*:

> Your shaykh is not someone from whom you hear, your shaykh is someone from whom you receive. Your shaykh is not someone whose expressions confront you, your shaykh is the one whose signals become secreted within you. Your shaykh is not he who calls you to the door, but he who removes the veil between himself and you. Your shaykh is not the one whose words challenge you, but he whose spiritual state uplifts you. Your shaykh is the one who releases you from the prison of your vain desires and brings you into the Presence of the Lord. Your shaykh is the one who never ceases to polish the mirror of your heart, until the lights of your Lord become manifest therein. He will encourage you towards God so that you will set off towards Him, and he will be with you until you arrive in His Presence. He will not cease to be by your side until he has cast you between His Hands and thrust you into the light of the Divine Presence. Then he will say, "Here you are and here is your Lord."

Ibn ʿAṭāʾ-Allāh also said, "Do not keep the company of one whose spiritual state does not uplift you and whose words do not lead you towards God." The Proof of Islam, Imam Abū Ḥāmid al-Ghazālī, may God have mercy on him, said:

> In the beginning of my affair, I used to deny the spiritual states of the righteous and the stations of the gnostics. Then I kept companionship with my shaykh (Yūsuf al-Nassāj). He did not cease polishing me with (the command to perform) strenuous exertions until I was favored with spiritual illuminations (*wāridāt*). I saw God the Exalted in a dream. He said to me, "O Abū Ḥāmid! Put down your self's preoccupations. Keep companionship with the Sufi folk. I have placed them within My satisfaction, and made them the locus of My gaze. They are those who have traded the two abodes for the love of Me." I said, "By Your Might! But what if I have less than good thoughts of them?" He said, "You have indeed (harbored such thoughts). What cuts you off from them is your being occupied with the love of the world. Leave the world aside while you remain well-regarded (in it), before you are forced out of it in humiliation. I have poured on you lights from the Holy Assembly." Then I woke up in a happy state and went to my shaykh and related to him my dream. He smiled and said, "O Abū Ḥāmid, such are our elementary learning boards (*alwāḥ*) in the beginning. But companionship with me will beautify your vision with the luster of permanence."[288]

In his *Iḥyā ʿulūm al-dīn*, Imam al-Ghazālī also said:

> The aspirant requires a shaykh and teacher to emulate and to guide him to the balanced way. The way (*sabīl*) of religion is obscure (*ghāmiḍ*), and the ways of Satan are numerous and apparent. Who does not have a shaykh to guide him, Satan leads him to his own paths. Who thus seeks the plain way of destruction with no sentinel, let him proceed alone with his thoughts and destroy himself. The independent one (*mustaqil*) by himself is like a tree that sprouts by itself because it agitates the neighbors. Even if it remains long enough to grow leaves, it does not bear fruit. The aspirant must cling to his shaykh and hold tightly to him.

288 This narration is excerpted from ʿAbd al-Bāqī Sarūr, *Shakhṣiyāt ṣūfiyya*.

Someone offered these Divine pearls of wisdom:

> There is no sweetness to life except the companionship of the Sufis (*fuqarā'*)
> They are sultans, lords, and princes
> Sitting with them in companionship is to acquire proper comportment
> The provision of your fortune, no matter where you have been before.

As for the question about seeking the shaykh: is it strictly incumbent (*farḍ*) on every single individual, or on some but not others, and what is the reason in either case? Our master, the Hidden Pole and the well-known Muḥammadan Seal Sīdī Aḥmad al-Tijani answered, as recorded in the book *Rawḍ al-muḥibb al-fānī* of Sīdī Muḥammad b. al-Mashrī:[289]

> The quest for the shaykh is not a duty imposed by the Sacred Law (*sharīʿa*), with the inevitable consequence of reward for its performance and punishment for its abandonment. There is nothing like that in the *Sharīʿa*, but it is obligatory from the perspective of common sense, just as the search for water is imperative for the thirsty person, for common sense tells him that he will perish or die if he doesn't find water to satisfy his thirst. Such a perspective relates to what has been mentioned, namely that human beings have only been created for the worship of God and the sole dedication to the Divine Presence, by the rejection of everything besides Him.
> The spiritual aspirant (*murīd*) has come to know his own inability to make his lower self (*nafs*) to comply with the requirements of entering the Divine Presence, and he has recognized the weakness of his own self in what is required to enter the Divine Presence in terms of fulfilling the necessary duties and proper modes of conduct (*adab*). He has come to know that he has no refuge or safety from God if he

289 This section also comprises a portion of the eighth chapter of Shaykh Ibrāhīm Niasse's *Kāshif al-ilbās*.

should remain attached to his lower self, following its vain passions and turning away from God the Exalted.

From this perspective, it is clearly necessary for him to seek out the complete shaykh. This necessity is strictly a matter of natural logic, not a ruling derived from legal texts, since what is mentioned in the legal texts is only the obligation to fulfill the rights of God, both inwardly and outwardly. This duty is an obligation on every single individual among His servants and no one has any legally valid excuse for neglecting it, nor has he any excuse for his subservience to vain desires and his inability to control his lower self.

There is nothing in the Sacred Law except the incumbency thereof, and the penalty incurred by violating the prohibition of neglecting that duty. This is what is contained in the *Sharīʿa*. The shaykh who must be sought is the shaykh who is qualified to provide such instruction, he being the one who teaches the nature of the legal observances demanded of the servant, in terms of performance of the commandments and avoidance of the prohibitions.

Every person ignorant (of God) must seek out the shaykh, for no one can do without him. Again, there is nothing other than this, from a legal perspective, that requires seeking out the shaykhs. But it is definitely an obligation from the perspective of common sense, since the ignorant person is comparable to the invalid. If such a person has resigned himself to sickness, on account of his inability to cure himself by his own means, one can only conclude that he wishes to remain sick. On the other hand, if the patient should ask how it is that he may obtain perfect, optimum health, one would tell him to seek out the expert physician. Indeed, the expert physician is familiar with the sickness and its cause, he knows the medicine that will cure it and he knows how this medicine should be applied, how much should be taken, in what manner, how often, and under what circumstances. May God's Peace be with you all.

The Comportment (*adab*) of the Perfected Actualized Gnostic Sages

The perfected shaykhs and the actualized gnostics are unanimously agreed that proper conduct (*adab*) on the path of God's people is most important in every matter. *Adab* is the confluence of all good and piousness. They have stipulated that it is necessary to journey the way of *adab* in everything. Who does so arrives and finds communion (with God). Who does not is cut off and dissociated (from God). The entire Sufi path is (nothing but) proper comportment (ādāb). For every time there is a proper conduct, for every state a conduct, and every station a conduct.

The Prophet, God's peace and blessing upon him, said, "My Lord trained me with the best conduct, and then ordained for me nobility of character (*akhlāq*)."

Conduct (*adab*) is the refinement of ones outward and inward self, and when this happens, a person becomes "well-mannered" (*adīb*). Ibn ʿArabī, may God be pleased with him, said, "All good is gathered in proper conduct."

Ibn ʿAṭā'-Allāh said, "Proper conduct means that you are occupied with commendable things." Someone asked him what he meant. He said: "It means that you practice proper conduct with God, in private and in public. If you do this, you will become well mannered, even if you do not speak Arabic." Then he recited:

> When we speak, what comes forth is only beauty
> And if we remain silent what comes forth is only beauty.

There is no more excellent speech than what some of the Sufis have said concerning proper conduct. (They said) Proper conduct (*adab*) is when the servant behaves with correct behavior, outwardly and inwardly. As for his outward self, he complies the Sacred Law (*sharīʿa*) and follows the Sunnah in his words and deeds. As for his inward self, he is in accord with the Reality (*al-ḥaqīqa*). He accepts and is pleased with what God desires of him. He sees that all blessing on him is from God the Exalted, whether it comes right away or is delayed. If it is immediate, this is the soul's attainment of what it loves right away. If it is delayed, this is indeed a type of detriment or calamity visited upon him because of his mistakes; but the blessing will return to him later on. By this expression, it is still a blessing. The possessor of such conduct is favored to only see blessing, which covers over any rancor. He witness the blessing of God the Exalted on him externally and internally.

In a prophetic narration on the authority of Muʿādh b. Jabal, may God be pleased with him, the Prophet, God's peace and blessing upon him, said: "Help Islam by having good character and beautiful comportment."

Anas ibn Malik, may God be pleased with him, is reported to have said, "Having good conduct while performing an action is a sign of the action being accepted (by God)."

ʿAbdallāh b. al-Mubārak, may God be pleased with him, said, "Whoever is negligent of good conduct, is punished with being deprived of the Prophetic behavioral ideal (*sunna*). Whoever is negligent of the *sunna*, is punished with being deprived of the legal incumbencies (*farāʾiḍ*). Whoever is negligent of the incumbencies, is punished with the deprivation of gnosis (*maʿrifa*)."

Dhū l-Nūn al-Miṣrī, may God be pleased with him, said: "If the aspirant (*murīd*) turns away from good conduct, he is sent back to whence he came."

As for the proper conduct with the spiritual guide (*shaykh*), it is to have firm conviction concerning his spiritual completion (*kamāl*), and (to not doubt) that he is among the folk of guidance and spiritual training, combining the Sacred Law (*sharīʿa*) and the Reality (*ḥaqīqa*), combining rapture (*jadhb*) with wayfaring (*sulūk*). (And to know) that he is in the footsteps of the Prophet, God's blessing and peace on him. Secondly, he must exalt him and guard his reverence (for God) in his absence as well as his presence. Spiritual training is by the love he has for him in his heart, and this love is the evidence of his truthfulness. Who is not truthful does not travel, even if he were to remain with the Shaykh for a thousand years. May God have mercy on Sīdī Muḥammad Sharqī, who said, "Who is not truthful, sells nothing with his boisterous shouting. Who does not rectify himself, does not pass through any door."

As for the proper comportment with the brethren, it was Ibn ʿAjība who mentioned: "Guard their honor whether they are present or absent. Do not slander anyone, and do not belittle anyone. Do not say, 'The companions of Sīdī so-and-so are perfected, while the companions of Sīdī so-and-so are wanting.' Or, 'So-and-so is a gnostic and so-and-so is not.' Or, 'So-and-so is weak (in faith), and so-and-so is strong.' Anything of this nature is the essence of calumny, and this is forbidden (*ḥarām*) by consensus, especially in the case of the saints. Their flesh is deadly poison, just as is the flesh of the scholars and the righteous. The aspirant is warned against this blameworthy trait and is warned to flee from its imprint as one would flee from the lion. Whoever is prone to this will never succeed. The saints are like the Prophets, and who differentiates between them restricts their goodness and denies their blessing. Some of the Sufis have said that whoever is exposed by the disciples cannot be consoled by the Shaykh, but whomever the Shaykh exposes is consoled by the disciples."

Part of good conduct with the brethren is also to offer counsel and fellowship, and to work with them according to the principle, "*And cooperate together in piety and God-consciousness.*"[290] The Shaykh of Islam, our Master al-Ḥājj Ibrāhīm said:

O seeker! You must have good conduct
It is indeed the door for every wayfarer.

And he said in the same poem:

Conduct yourself properly externally and internally
With this does one ascend to high positions.

Bewilderment and Surrender

In bewilderment and surrender to God is found complete faith that does not depend on tradition (*taqlīd*) and which is not satisfied by derived evidence alone. This faith depends on illuminated vision by which is witnessed the eternal Divine Presence. Such a person witnesses this Presence in all of his actions, movements, and stillness.

290 Qur'ān, 5:2.

Long ago, one of the distinguished folk said, "No one knows God except that He makes Himself known to him. No one witnesses the Divine Oneness, unless the Divine Oneness is made witness to him. No one believes in Him except He is kind to him. No one is purified except God manifests in his inner most being. No one is made sincere except God attracts him to Him. No one is made righteous except God creates this righteousness for him."

And it is said that the creation is only able to describe the Creator with the tongue of incapacity, which is why the Prophet, God's peace and blessing upon him, said, "I cannot enumerate the ways of praising You! You are as You have praised Yourself!" This was narrated in Muslim and in other *ḥadīth* collections.

It has been narrated by al-Tirmidhī in *Nawādir al-uṣūl*, "God the Most High has concealed Himself from the faculties of the intellect (ʿuqūl), just as He concealed Himself from the eyes (*abṣār*), and the heavenly hosts seek Him just as you seek Him." This is why al-Junayd said, "The ending point of the intellect is bewilderment (*ḥayra*)." Dhū l-Nūn al-Miṣrī said, "The utmost degree of the gnostics is bewilderment."

God the Exalted said, "*God warns you all of Himself, and God is Compassionate with His servants.*"[291]

And He said, "*They have not given God a just estimation of His power.*"[292]

And He said, "*He knows what is before them and behind them, and they have not gauged the extent of His knowledge.*"[293]

And He said, "*And they do understand the smallest fragment of His knowledge except as He wills.*"[294]

And He said, "*Do not pursue that of which you have no knowledge. Indeed, the hearing, sight, and heart, will all be held to account.*"[295]

And He said, "*Say, My Lord has only forbidden indecencies, such of them as are apparent and such as are hidden, and sin and wrongful oppression, and that you associate with God that for which He has not*

---

291 Qur'ān, 3:30.

292 Qur'ān, 22:74.

293 Qur'ān, 20:110.

294 Qur'ān, 2:255.

295 Qur'ān, 17:36.

sent down authority, and that you say about God that which you do not know."[296]

And He said, *"Glorious is your Lord, the Lord of Might, above what they (falsely) attribute to Him."*[297]

All of this demonstrates that the created entities, whatever they are, cannot delimit the Creator. They cannot comprehend Him by expression, for His Essential Being is free from specification. The one who is able to comprehend God is none but God Himself, none other. Human minds are weak and limited and cannot understand Divine Oneness (*tawḥīd*) and gnosis, except that a created thing is in need of a creator. This is why God has not overburdened the mind with the incumbency of understanding Him. It is enough that mankind submits and believes in Him. Imam al-Buṣayrī said:

> He did not try us with things that baffle the mind
> Such was His concern for us, so we neither doubted nor strayed.

From all of this we understand that gnosis is an activity of the heart, not of the mind. This is why Abū Bakr al-Ṣaddīq, may God be pleased with him, said, "The incapacity to attain realization is itself a realization." Also in this meaning, the consummate scholar Muḥammad Fāl wuld Matālī said:

> Plunging into comprehending Him is associating partners with Him
> The incapacity in comprehending Him is itself a realization
> The incapacity in comprehending Him is (the station) of (Abū Bakr) the truthful
> For he said this was itself the comprehension and the realization.

---

296 Qur'ān, 7:33.

297 Qur'ān, 37:180.

The Veil (*al-ḥijāb*)

The Prophet, peace and blessings of God be upon him, said, "God has 70,000 veils of light and darkness. If He were to remove them, the radiant splendor of His Countenance would burn up whoever met His Gaze." I would add that the folk of God are unanimous in agreement that the "veils" are in relation to the servant, not the Real, Glorified and Exalted is He. The proof for this is the fact that nothing actually veils the Countenance of God. He continually manifests Himself to the creation, with a manifestation that is direct and immediate, from the first act of creation. Nothing has been burned from that manifestation. So, were there veils for Him then the entire Cosmos would have been burned with just one glance from Him, as mentioned in the *ḥadīth*. Understand this well! The "greatest Shaykh" Imam Muḥyī l-Dīn Ibn al-ʿArabī said in his book *al-Ḥujub*:

> O lover, whoever you are, know that the veils between you and your beloved, whomever it is, are nothing except your tarrying with (other) things, the things are not veils themselves. It has been said to the one who has not "tasted" the flavor of the spiritual realities: you have tarried with created things because of the shortcoming of your perception; that is, a lack of penetration, expressed by the term "veil" (*ḥijāb*). The veil itself is nonexistent, and in nonexistence (*al-ʿadam*) there is absolutely nothing, and certainly no veil. If there were actually veils, whoever became veiled from you, would also have been veiled (in otherness). As for the gnostic, for whom the Real has become his hearing and sight, this one knows what is meant by "veil."

Know that if you have become completely preoccupied with a matter, you necessarily have become delayed with it. This stopping is your veil, for stopping with the creation veils you from the Real, while stopping with the Real veils you from the creation. This is the (difference between) extension (of the self into the world) and (Divine) intimacy, mentioned in the Qurʾan and the *Sunna* as darkness and illuminated love. The veils become constructed on the basis of this worldly self-extension.

Ibn ʿAjība said in Īqāẓ al-himam: "The Real is not veiled from you, rather it is you who are veiled from seeing Him, for were there anything to veil Him, then that which veils Him would cover Him, and if He were covered then that would be a limitation to His Being, and if something contained something else it overpowers it. '*And He is the Omnipotent, overpowering His servants.*'"[298]

I would add that veiling is inconceivable for the reality of the Real, exalted is He, for nothing veils Him. He is Manifest by everything, before everything, after everything. Nothing else is manifest with Him, and there is no existence in reality except for Him. He is not veiled from you, rather it is you who are veiled from seeing Him by your belief in otherness and the attachment of your heart to sensory affairs. If your heart were completely devoted to seeking the Lord, you would have refused to see anything else. You would have seen the Light of the Real shining brightly in the manifestations of Being. What was veiled from you in fleeting illusion would have become witnessed directly.

In this meaning, Ibn ʿAṭā'-Allāh said, "The Real did not veil Himself from you by some reality coexisting with Him, since there is no reality other than Him. What veils Him from you is nothing but the illusion that something is existing with Him." One of the Sufi poets said:

> You are not unveiled except by lifting the veil, then
> Extraordinary is that Your appearance could ever have been covered.

Another poet said:

> She appeared, she is not hidden from anyone
> Except from the one born blind, unable to see the moon
> She only hid herself with what appeared as a veil
> How to know Him who became concealed by Might?

298 Qur'ān, 6:18.

Ibn ʿAjība also said in the Īqāẓ al-himam: "The Most High became veiled in His state of appearance. This is evidence of the existence of his omnipotence, as was pointed out in the *Ḥikam* (of Ibn ʿAṭāʾ-Allāh) with the words, 'Among the evidence for the existence of His omnipotence (*qahr*), glorious is He, is that He veils you from Him with what has no existence with Him.'"

God veiled Himself from the creation with things that do not exist. They are illusions, and illusions do not exist, they lack reality. What veils Him is the intensity of His appearance. And the vision is not prevented from seeing Him except by the overpowering nature of His Light. God is alone in the existence, for there is nothing existing with God.

The Most High said, "*Everything is perishing (hālik) except His Countenance.*"[299] And the verbal noun (*hālik*) is in reality the expression of a permanent condition.

And the Most High said, "*He is the First, the Last, the Manifest, the Hidden.*"[300]

And God said, "*Wherever you turn, there is the Face of God.*"[301]

And God said, "*He is with you wherever you are.*"[302]

And God said, "*We told you that your Lord is all around mankind.*"[303]

And God said, "*And you (Muḥammad) did not throw when you threw, but God was He who threw.*"[304]

And God said, "*Surely those who pledged allegiance to you (Muḥammad), pledged allegiance to God.*"[305]

The Prophet, God's blessing and peace on him, said, "The best words spoken by a poet were those of Labīd, "Surely everything other than God is falsehood (*bāṭil*), and every (worldly) blessing is illusionary, perishing."

And the Prophet, God's blessing and peace on him, said, "God says, 'O My servants! I was sick and you did not visit Me.' They say, 'O Lord!

299 Qur'ān, 28:88
300 Qur'ān, 57:3.
301 Qur'ān, 2:115.
302 Qur'ān, 57:4.
303 Qur'ān, 17:60.
304 Qur'ān, 8:17.
305 Qur'ān, 48:10.

How can we visit You, the Lord of the worlds?' God says, 'When my servant so-and-so became ill, you did not visit him. If you had visited him, you would have found Me with him.'" This *ḥadīth* is an indication that these (creations) are but lifeless skeletons, and people are phantoms without any reality belonging to themselves. They are like shadows.

Our master, the Shaykh of Islam, Shaykh Ibrāhīm Niasse quoted from Shaykh al-Tijānī in the book *Kāshif al-ilbās* to explain the removal of the veil.

> The removal of the veil is dependent on quickly detaching oneself from worldly and carnal lusts, desisting from esteeming worldly benefits and from their impatient procurement. The harmful effects of worldly attachment can be prevented by gracious and gentle asceticism (*zuhd*), rather than complete renunciation or abstinence. Veiling is caused by excessive eating, drinking, socializing, talking, sleeping and continual heedlessness of the remembrance of God, Exalted is He. The veils is removed by hunger and thirst in gentle moderation, removing oneself from social mixing, persistent absolute silence except in rare cases of necessity, keeping the night vigil in gentle moderation, and constant remembrance of God with the heart and tongue, unceasingly and with any form of remembrance.
>
> The types of remembrance that remove the veils include those that tear away the veil from the spirit completely and those that are partially effective, removing a veil of a particular kind. The remembrances which are totally effective are the following: *lā ilāha ill-Allāh* or *Ṣalāt 'ala l-Nabbī* or *Subḥān-Allāh* or *al-Ḥamdu li-Llāh* or *Allāhu Akbar* or *Bismi-Llāh al-Raḥmān al-Raḥīm* or *Allāh Allāh Allāh* or *Allāhu lā ilāha illa Huwa l-Ḥayy al-Qayyūm.*
>
> The remembrances that are partially effective include the rest of the Beautiful Names of God. Each Name removes one type of veil, but it does not apply to another. And the success is with God, Most High.

Shaykh Ibrāhīm said, "These words of his are worthy of being inscribed with golden ink! If someone wants more information on how to tear away the veils, in addition to what has been provided here, let him keep company with the distinguished experts on the subject." He continued:

Sīdī al-ʿArabī b. al-Sā'iḥ,[306] may God be pleased with him, said, "The *Jawāhir al-maʿānī* contains numerous methods, all of them leading to God the Exalted." I would point out that more has been concealed than what has been made public. The Director of Fortune directs some people, while the Divine Averter misguides others. As one poet said: "The rain pours down and the earth becomes green, whether the seeker of goodness settles there or leaves."

Entering the Holy Presence

Ibn ʿAjība said: "The Divine Presence is a most sanctified and exalted presence, and no one enters it except the purified. It is prohibited for the impure heart to enter the mosque of the Divine Presence, and the filth of the heart is its heedless of its Lord."

The Most High said: "*O you who believe, do not approach the prayer while you are intoxicated, until you know what you are saying, and [do not approach] while in a state of ritual impurity, except while traveling, until you have cleansed yourselves.*"[307]

"In other words, do not approach worship in the Divine Presence while you are drunk with the love of the world and the vision of otherness, until you wake up and reflect on what you are saying in the Presence of the Sovereign Lord. And do not come with the filth of heedlessness and the vision of otherness until you are cleansed with the water of the unseen. Ibn ʿArabī al-Ḥātimī was referring to this when he said:[308]

Purify yourself with the water of the unseen if you would possess a secret

If not, make the dry ablution (*tayammum*) with dust or stone

---

306 Muḥammad al-ʿArabī b. al-Sā'iḥ (d. 1898, Rabat), author of the seminal text *Bughyat al-mustafīd,* was among the most eminent scholars of the Tijāniyya in the latter half of the nineteenth century. See Wright, *Realizing Islam*, 13.

307 Qur'ān, 4:43.

308 The following verses are sometimes also attributed to Junayd al-Baghdadi.

Put forth an Imam in front of you
    And pray the dawn prayer in the beginning of its time
This is the prayer of the knowledgeable of their Lord
    If you are among them, come quench the dry land with the ocean.

"In other words, purify yourself from the vision of your lower-self (*nafs*) with the water of the unseen, the vision of your Lord. Or in other words, purify yourself from the vision of the senses to the vision of the meaning. Or: purify yourself from seeing the seen world with the water of seeing the unseen world. Or: purify yourself from the vision of otherness with the water of gnosis. He is surely hidden from you by everything other than Him, but if you cleanse yourself from the witness of otherness, you will have cleansed yourself from all defects."

Some time ago, I wrote the following verses similar to this in meaning:

I found my goal after the denial of everything other than Him
    He is the One, the Near to all of His creation
There is nothing besides the Real in every single place
    So let the one desiring arrival contemplate the achievement of his arrival.

Qur'an Verses and Prophetic Statements explaining Gnosis

The Most High said: "*God is the Light of the heavens and the earth. The similitude of His light is as a niche wherein is a lamp. The lamp is in a glass, the glass, is as it were a glittering star, lit from a blessed tree, an olive, neither of the east, nor of the west, whose oil would almost glow forth, even if no fire touched it. Light upon light. God guides whom He will to His light; and God sets forth parables to mankind, for God is knower of all things.*

In the houses which God has allowed to be raised up, that His Name may therein be remembered. In them is He glorified morning and evening.

People whom neither merchandise nor sale distract them from the remembrance of God, and from the observance of prayer, and paying to the poor their due. This because they fear a day when hearts and eyes will be turned about.

That God may recompense them for the best of what they did and increase reward for them of His bounty. God provides for whom He wills without measure."[309]

Some of those of knowledge have said that God here explained the reality that He has a general, comprehensive Light (*nūr ʿām*) by which He has illuminated the heavens and earth. By this Light existence (*wujūd*) was manifested from a state of non-manifestation. [The emphasis on light is appropriate because] the idea that the manifestation of something by something else is in effect a claim of existence for the thing manifested in and of itself. God is the Manifest by His Essential Being, the (apparent) manifestation of other than Him is (only) the Light: and He is the Light that manifested the heavens and the earth through His illumination. But where ordinary lights make dense bodies appear to the senses by shining upon them, the manifestation of things from the Divine Light is different. The Divine Light is the essence of their existence, whereas the sensory light's illumination of dense bodies does not mean that it is the source of their existence.

There is also a special light (*nūr khāṣṣ*) by which He enlightens the believers and guides them to Him through their righteous deeds. That is the light of gnosis (*maʿrifa*) by which He enlightens their hearts and their vision (on) "*a day when hearts and eyes will be turned about.*" They are guided by this light to their eternal happiness. In this light they witness with their eyes what had been hidden from them in the material world (*dunyā*). The Most High compared this light to a lamp inside of a glass inside of a niche, lit from an oil of utmost purity. The glass gleams as if it were a glittering star. So light is added upon light. The lamp is placed in the houses of worship, in which God is glorified by believers who are not distracted from the remembrance and worship of their Lord by buying and selling.

---

309 Qur'an, 24:35-38. The translation here mostly follows that of Ali Özek, *The Glorious Qur'an* (Istanbul: Asyr Media, 1995).

This is a description of how God has honored the believers with the light of knowing Him, those in pursuit of eternal happiness. He has forbidden the deniers (*kāfirūn*) from this light, and He has left them in the darkness where they cannot see. God has favored whoever occupies himself with his Lord, turning away from the exhibition of the life of this world through a light from His presence. And God does what He wills. To Him belong the sovereignty and the final destination.

Concerning the words of the Most High, "*And they have not appraised of God a true appraisal,*"[310] al-Akhfash[311] said: "It means they have not known Him with true gnosis."

Consider the words of the Messenger, God's peace and blessing upon him: "Who knows himself, knows his Lord." Muḥyī al-Dīn Ibn ʿArabī said on the basis of this *ḥadīth*: "He, the peace and blessing of God on him, was indicating with these words that you are not you. Rather, you are Him in the negation (*bilā*) of you. He is not inside you, nor is He removed from you. And you are not removed from Him, nor are you inside of Him. This does not mean that you exist, or that your description is fixed by sufficiency in Him. Since you were once nothing, you are not presently anything, not by your own self, not in Him, not with Him. You are neither passing out of existence, nor do you exist. You are He, and He is you, without any reason to explain. If you have come to know that your existence is defined like this, you have come to know God. If not, then not."

The Prophet, God's peace and blessing upon him, said on the authority of ʿĀʾisha, may God be pleased with her: "The support of the house is its foundation. The support of the religion is the knowledge (*maʿrifa*) of God Most High, certainty, and the restrained mind." (He was asked) "What is the restrained mind?" He said, "The cessation from the disobedience to God, and the guarding of the obedience to God."[312] The Prophet also said, "Who is pleased with God as his Lord, Islam as his religion, and

---

310 Qurʾān, 6:91.

311 The translator has not been able to identify this name, but it might be ʿAbd al-Ḥamīd al-Akhfash al-Akbar (d. 793), a famous Arabic grammarian who lived in Basra, Iraq.

312 Ḥadīth related by Imam Daylamī.

Muḥammad, God's blessing and peace on him, as his Prophet, has tasted (*dhāq*) the sweetness of faith."[313] One poet said:

A sun rose from a most beloved night
    Illuminating what was hidden
The sun of daylight is obscured by the night
    But the sun of the hearts is never absent.

A gnostic said:

I saw my Lord with the eye of my heart
    I said, there is no doubt You are You.

Another poet said:

When I saw God, I did not see anything other
    With us, otherness is forbidden.

The Claim of the Cessation of Spiritual Training in the earlier generations and the Response of Shaykh Ibrāhīm Niasse, *Ṣāḥib al-Fayḍa*

The allegation that spiritual training has been truncated in our time is nothing new. Some said the same in previous times, and some still repeat the claim despite the conclusive proofs with which our scholars have refuted their claims. Some even go so far as to claim the cessation of sainthood, and other things besides. Our Master the Shaykh of Islam, the bringer of the Tijānī flood, Shaykh Ibrāhīm b. al-Ḥājj ʿAbdallāh Niasse spoke about this issue in his book, *Kāshif al-ilbās*. We will include the gist of his words on the subject here:[314]

313 The word "taste" (*dhawq*) is the same used by Sufis to describe the necessity of "tasting," or direct experience of spiritual realities.

314 The following section is excerpted from Shaykh Ibrāhīm Niasse, *The Removal of Confusion Concerning the Flood of the Saint Seal Aḥmad al-Tijani* (Fons Vitae, 2010), 1-16.

According to Sidi (Aḥmad) Zarrūq,[315] in the book *Ta'sīs al-Qawā'id*: "Our Shaykh Abū l-'Abbās al-Ḥaḍramī said: 'Spiritual training (*tarbiya*) in the technical sense has ceased to be practiced, and all that remains is training by spiritual zeal (*himma*) and state (*ḥāl*). It is thus incumbent on you to follow the Qur'ān and the Sunnah, without addition or subtraction.'" The rest of this quotation will be presented later. But let us say here that this statement, made in the ninth century after the Hijra (sixteenth century of the Common Era), should not be understood, especially by the one deprived of spiritual experience and gnosis, as meaning that spiritual training has ceased absolutely. Neither Zarrūq nor his Shaykh al-Ḥaḍramī meant this.

The actual meaning intended was explained by the erudite scholar Ibn 'Ajība in his *Īqāẓ al-Himam*:

> Some might hold to the literal meaning of al-Ḥaḍramī's words: "Spiritual training in the technical sense has ceased to be practiced, and all that remains is training by spiritual zeal and state. Thus, it is incumbent on you to follow the Qur'ān and the *Sunna*." My response to this is as follows: Al-Ḥaḍramī did not mean to say that the cessation of spiritual training will last for all eternity. Far be it from al-Ḥaḍramī to pass such judgment on God and limit His Power! What he meant was that there were many impostors and pretenders in his time, so he warned his contemporaries to beware of them. The high erudition of al-Ḥaḍramī and Zarrūq is inconsistent with the literal meaning of their words. Even if they are held to the literal meaning, that spiritual training had ceased for all eternity, they are surely not infallible. Every statement, theirs included, is subject to critical evaluation, except for the statement of our Prophet, God's blessing and peace on him. Indeed, following the time of al-Ḥaḍramī, an innumerable number of distinguished Sufi scholars have been carrying out orthodox spiritual training by means of spiritual states (*ḥāl*), spoken words (*maqāl*), and zeal

315 Sidi Aḥmad Zarrūq al-Burnusi al-Fasi (d. 1493) was a North African scholarly Sufi of the Shādhilī order.

> (*himma*). They also exist in this time of ours, famous like radiant beacons. God has guided many of the creation with their assistance, and with their help He has taught the saints what no one knows, except those whom God has blessed.

Ibn ʿAjība's explanation is proven by the appearance of Shaykh Aḥmad al-Tijānī, the Seal of Saints and the standard-bearer of spiritual training well after the ninth-century statements of al-Ḥaḍramī and his student. Shaykh al-Tijānī's role as a spiritual trainer cannot be doubted by anyone endowed with the slightest faith and submission to him. The same is true of Shaykh al-Sayyid al-Mukhtār al-Kuntī,[316] as well as the perfected ones who were trained by such men, and thereby attained to the highest rank of those shaykhs providing spiritual training (*tarbiya*) and elevation (*tarqiya*).

Our Shaykh and means of access to our Lord, Shaykh Aḥmad al-Tijānī, Seal of the Saints, may God be pleased with him, has demonstrated that among the people of his Spiritual Path are the masters of spiritual training (*mashāʾikh al-tarbiya*). This is indicated by his authentic statements recorded in the *Jāmiʿ*:[317]

> (He said) "If God grants illumination (*fatḥ*) to my companions, the one among them who sits in my presence, in the town where I am, will fear his own destruction (*halāk*)." One of his companions asked him, "Is this from you, or from God?" To this he replied, "It is from God, without my having a choice in the matter." He mentioned this on the second Sunday of the sacred month of Sha'ban, in the year 1223 of the Hijra (1808 C.E.). Then he said on the next Monday: "The fear that was mentioned is for the one among my companions who has been authorized with the power of Divine disposition (*taṣarruf*), and to provide his fellow creatures with spiritual training (*tarbiya*)."

---

316 Al-Mukhtār al-Kuntī (d. 1811) lived near Timbuktu, Mali, and revived the Qādiriyya in West Africa.

317 The *Kitāb al-Jāmiʿ li al-ʿUlūm al-Fāʾida min Biḥār al-Quṭb al-Maktūm* is one of the primary sources of the Tijānī order, written during the founder's lifetime in 1808 by Muḥammad b. al-Mishrī.

The complete statement of Sidi Zarrūq in *Ta'sīs al-Qawā'id* partially quoted earlier reads as follows:

> We conclude with the statement of our Shaykh Abū l-ʿAbbās al-Ḥaḍramī: "Spiritual training (*tarbiya*) in the technical sense has ceased to be practiced, and all that remains is training by spiritual zeal (*himma*) and state (*ḥāl*). It is thus incumbent on you to follow the Qur'ān and the *Sunna*, without addition or subtraction. This applies to one's dealing with the Real (*al-Ḥaqq*), with one's own self (*nafs*), and with the creation.
>
> "Three things must be observed in one's relationship to the Real: the performance of obligatory duties, the avoidance of forbidden things, and the submission to the rule of the Sacred Law.
>
> "Three things also must be observed in dealing with one's ego-self (*nafs*): moderation, refraining from exciting it, guarding against its mischievous impulses toward (arbitrary) attraction and repulsion, acceptance and rejection, approach and retreat.
>
> "There are also three things to observe in one's relationship with the creation: providing their rightful dues, withholding oneself from their possessions, and eschewing that which disturbs their hearts, except in the unavoidable case of genuine necessity.
>
> "The aspirant (*murīd*) is doomed to destruction and failure if he should manifest any of the following: ostentation; a desire to influence the general administration of affairs; taking it on himself to correct the reprehensible behavior of the general public; preoccupation with Holy War (*jihād*), while neglecting other virtues; wanting to monopolize all merits for himself; seeking out the imperfections of his fellow brothers; preoccupation with warning others; acting on hearsay; participating in social gatherings with neither the intention to learn nor to teach; mixing with worldly leaders under the pretext of religious devotion; preoccupation with subtle intricacies (of the religion), rather than actual practice to rectify his faults; undertaking spiritual training (*tarbiya*) without authorization (*taqdīm*) from a shaykh, imam or scholar; following any and every person, the one speaking truth and the one speaking falsehood, without distinguishing their

spiritual states; looking down on those connected to God, and assuming their insincerity because of what he sees in them; fondness for special permissions and ambiguous interpretations; preferring the hidden (*bāṭin*) to the apparent (*ẓāhir*), or remaining content with the apparent without reference to the hidden, or concluding something from one incompatible with the other; being satisfied with knowledge without practice, or practice without knowledge or reference to the spiritual state (*ḥāl*), or spiritual state without knowledge or practice; non-substantiation of his knowledge, practice, spiritual state or religious conviction in the sources of the Muslim community, such as the books of Ibn ʿAtāʾ-Allāh concerning esoteric knowledge, especially the *Tanwīr*,[318] or the *Madkhal* of Ibn al-Ḥājj[319] concerning exoteric knowledge, or the book of his Shaykh Ibn Abī Jamra,[320] and the works of the scholars who followed them. But if such an aspirant accepts the teachings of these authorities, he will be saved as a Muslim, if God wills. Virtuousness and success are from God.

"God's Messenger, the blessing and peace of God on him, was asked about the verse of the Qur'ān: 'O you who believe! Guard your own souls!' (5:105). He replied, 'When you see greedy lust being obeyed, passionate desire being pursued, and every holder of an opinion taking conceited pride in his opinion; be on special guard for your own soul (*nafs*)'[321] He also related a statement from the Scrolls of Abraham (*ṣuḥuf Ibrāhīm*):

> The intelligent person should be aware of his age (*zaman*), hold his tongue and mind his business. The intelligent one should

---

318 Ibn ʿAṭāʾ-Allāh al-Iskandarī (d. 1309), *Kitāb al-Tanwīr fī Isāt al-Tadbīr* has been described as the "basic training manual for Sufis in North Africa." It has been translated by Scott Kugle, *The Book of Illumination* (Fons Vitae, 2005).

319 Muḥammad b. al-Ḥājj al-Abdarī al-Fāsī (d. 1336) taught at the Qayrawin University in Fes, Morocco, but traveled throughout North Africa and is buried in Egypt. His work, *Madkhal al-Shara al-Sharīf ʿala al-Madhāhib* is a four-volume work discussing various points of Islamic law.

320 Ibn Abī Jamra (d. 1300) was a renowned Ḥadīth scholar and jurist of the Maliki school, originally from Andalusia but who settled in Cairo. His major work was *Bahjat al-Nufūs*, which is a commentary on *Ṣaḥīḥ Bukhārī*.

321 Reported by Abū Dāwūd in his *Sunan*, by Imam al-Tirmidhī in his *Sunan*, and by Ibn Mājah in his *Sunan*.

> also hold on to four times: a time in which he calls himself to account; a time when he confides in his Lord; a time in which he spends with his brothers, the ones who make him aware of his faults and guide him toward his Lord; and a time in which he allows himself to enjoy permissible desires.

> May God provide us with this and help us in it. May He enable us and our companions to benefit thereby, for we are helpless without Him! He is sufficient for us, an excellent Custodian. May God bless our Master, Prophet and Patron, Muḥammad, and peace upon his family and companions."

Careful study of Shaykh Abū l-ʿAbbās al-Ḥaḍramī's above statement reveals its true meaning. This is why the gnostic of God, al-Sayyid al-ʿArabī b. al-Sā'iḥ explained:

> The meaning of spiritual training (*tarbiya*) in this context (alluded to by Zarrūq) is spiritual training in the technical sense, which was developed after the first three centuries (following the Prophet). This is the spiritual training which Shaykh Zarrūq believed, on the authority of some of his masters, had ceased to be practiced. He was followed in this regard by the scholarly researcher al-Yūsī,[322] may God have mercy on him, who said: "In the opinion of al-Ḥaḍramī and Zarrūq, the meaning was not that spiritual training has ceased in the sense of providing guidance based on the Qur'ān and the *Sunna*, and the teaching of remembrance (*dhikr*). Nor did it mean the end of removing falsehood from the soul, ridding it of attachments and distractions, with the support and spiritual zeal of the shaykh. Indeed, this (role of the shaykh) is by the permission he receives in his innermost being from the Presence of God, or from the Presence of His Messenger, either in a state of wakefulness or sleep. Far be it from the people of God to

322 Abū 'Alī al-Hassan b. Mas'ud al-Yusi (d. 1691) was one of the more famous Moroccan Sufis of the seventeenth century. He was associated with the Nasiriyya branch of the Shadhiliyya Sufi order and authored numerous works covering a range of Islamic sciences. For more information, see Jacques Berque, *Al-Yousi: Problèmes de la Culture Marocaine au 17e Siècle* (Paris, 1958).

think (such training has ceased)!" For more on this subject, consult *al-Dhahab al-Ibrīz*.[323]

There are several Qur'ān verses and Prophetic traditions which contain indi-cations and glad tidings concerning this group (*ṭā'ifa*) manifestly committed to the Truth. And they are not limited to a particular time or place. For example, God the Exalted said: "*And among those whom We have created there is a community who guide with the Truth and establish justice therewith.*"[324] In his marginal commentary on the *Jalālayn*, the scholarly gnostic, Shaykh Sīdī al-Ṣāwī[325] said of this verse: "They are the community of Muḥammad, God's peace and blessing on him, since in a Prophetic tradition he said: 'A group from my community will not cease being committed to the Truth, until God's (final) command arrives.'"[326] Mu'āwiya once said while delivering a sermon: "I once heard God's Messenger say, 'Among my community there will never cease being a group obedient to God's command. They will not be harmed by those who forsake or oppose them, until God's (final) command arrives while they are committed to this.'"[327]

This group is not limited to any particular time, or to any particular location. Indeed, they are present in every place and time, for Islam always will be raised high and never be surpassed. The wanton sinners and purveyors of evil, however many they are, bear no consequence (on the ascendency of Islam). This is glad tidings for the community of Muḥammad, making it known that Islam and the Muslims are endowed with sublimity and honor until the Day of Resurrection draws near.

---

323 *Al-Dhahab al-Ibrīz* was written in 1720 by Aḥmad al-Lamati, the disciple of the aforementioned Shaykh 'Abd al-'Azīz al-Dabbāg. The work has remained extremely influential around the Muslim world ever since, and is one of the sources for emergence of the *Tariqa Muḥammadiyya* phenomenon since the late 18th century. For a translation see John O'Kane and Bernd Radtke, *Pure God from the Words of Sayyidi Abd al-Aziz al-Dabbagh: Al-Dhahab al-Ibriz min Kalam Sayyidi Abd al-Aziz al-Dabbagh* (Brill, 2007).

324 Qur'ān, 7:181.

325 Aḥmad al-Ṣāwī (d. 1825) was an important Indian scholar of the Maliki school of jurisprudence (*madhhab*) who wrote a commentary (*ḥāshiya*) on the *Tafsīr al-Jalālayn* of Jalāl al-Dīn al-Suyūṭī and Jalāl al-Dīn al-Maḥallī.

326 Reported by Imam al-Bukhārī in his *Ṣaḥīḥ*, by Imam Muslim in his *Ṣaḥīḥ*, by Abū Dāwūd in his *Sunan*, by al-Tirmidhī in his *Sunan*, and by Aḥmad b. Hanbal in his *Musnad*.

327 Ḥadīth reported in the collections of Muslim and Abū Dāwūd.

At this point, the bearers of the Qur'ān and the religious scholars will die. The Qur'ān will be erased from the books. A gentle wind will blow, and all in whom there is a tiny speck of faith with die. And this will not happen until after the (return and) death of Jesus, peace be upon him. Jesus will not die until after he slays the Antichrist (*al-Dajjāl*) and lives for forty years, as the Prophetic traditions have repeatedly confirmed. The Antichrist will not come seven years after the Mahdī, at the head of a (new) century.

One narration reports the Prophet's words: "There will always be a group in the West (*al-Maghrib*) ..."[328] Muḥyī al-Dīn Ibn al-ʿArabī al-Ḥātimī explained, "God placed the station of the Seal (*al-khatmiyya*) and Concealment (*al-katmiyya*) in Morocco (*al-Maghrib*), for that is the place of secrets and concealment." For more on this, consult Ibn al-ʿArabī's *al-Futūḥāt* (*al-Makkiyya*) and his *ʿAnqāʾ Mughrib fī Khatm al-Awliyāʾ wa shams al-Maghrib*. See also the *Bughyat* (*al-Mustafīd* of Muḥammad al-ʿArabī b. al-Sā'iḥ).

God the Exalted has said: "*A multitude from the earlier generations, and a multitude from the later generations.*"[329] Ibn 'Abbās reported that God's Messenger, God's blessing and peace on him, said: "The two multitudes are from my community."[330] This is found in *al-Jawāhir al-Ḥisān*.[331] According to Shihāb al-Dīn al-Khafājī in *Nasīm al-Riyāḍ*:[332]

> The Prophet's saying, "The best of you belong to my generation, then those who will follow them, then those who will follow

328 The full version of this Ḥadīth, found in *Ṣaḥīḥ Muslim* on the authority of Abū Hurayra: "The people of the West (*al-Maghrib*) will remain manifestly committed to the Truth, they will not be harmed by those who go against them or forsake them until the Final Hour." Imam Aḥmad b. Hanbal considered this to refer to the people of Shām (Syria), but other scholars considered this to refer to North Africa, as *al-Maghrib* is the Arabic name for Morocco. Certainly this latter opinion was held by Ibn al-'Arabī.

329 Qur'ān, 56:39-40.

330 Reported by Imam Ibn Jarīr al-Ṭabarī in his *Tafsīr*, and cited by Imam al-Haythami in *Majma' al-Zawā'id wa Mamba' al-Fawā'id*.

331 This is the multi-volume Qur'ān exegesis, *Jawāhir al-Ḥisān fī Tafsīr al-Qur'ān*, by Abd al-Raḥmān al-Tha'alibi (d. 1471).

332 This is the *Nasīm al-Riyāḍ fī sharḥ Shifā' al-Qāḍī Īyād*, a commentary on the *Shifā'* of Qadi Iyad (work of Ḥadīth and Prophetic biography from the 12th century) by the Egyptian Hanafi scholar Shihāb al-Dīn al-Khafājī (d. 1659).

> them,"[333] is not inconsistent with his saying, "My community is like the rain, for it is not known whether the best is in its first part or in its last." [334] The first part comes in one valley, and the last comes in another; meaning that somebody may come in this community (of Muḥammad) who provides people with tremendous benefit, beyond the means of anyone who preceded him. The first rain refers to particular individuals (from the earlier generations), while the second rain refers to the complete span of time (comprising the later generations); and indeed, what a difference there is between the two (for individuals to equal the whole span of time)!

Shaykh Zarrūq, may God be pleased with him, said in *Ta'sīs al-Qawā'id*:

> The preferential regard for certain times and people is a vestige of pagan ignorance and has no legal foundation. Thus the unbelievers said, *"If only this Qur'ān had been revealed to some great man from the two towns."*[335] So God the Exalted responded to them with His saying, *"Are they the ones who apportion the mercy of your Lord?"*[336] And when they said, *"We found our fathers following a religion, and we are guided by their footprints,"*[337] God responded to them by saying, *"(The one sent to warn them) said: 'What, even though I bring you better guidance than what you found your fathers following?'"*[338]
>
> It is necessary to consider the universality of God's gracious favor (*faḍl*), without regard for a certain time or an individual, except in the case of someone specifically distinguished by the Word of the Most High. In this respect (of being distinguished by God), the saints

333 Reported by al-Bukhārī in his *Ṣaḥīḥ*, by Imam Muslim in his *Ṣaḥīḥ*, by al-Nasā'ī in his *Sunan*, by Aḥmad in his *Musnad*, by al-Ṭaḥāwī in *Sharḥ Ma'āni al-Āthār*, and by al-Ṭabarānī in *al-Mu'jam al-Kabīr*.

334 Reported by al-Tirmidhī in his *Sunan* and by Aḥmad b. Hanbal in his *Musnad*.

335 Qur'ān, 43:31. The "two towns" referred to here are the main cities of Arabia at the time: Mecca and Yathrib (later called Medina).

336 Qur'ān, 43:32.

337 Qur'ān, 43:22.

338 Qur'ān, 43:24.

> follow the Prophets; for the saintly miracle (*karāma*) bears witness to the Prophetic miracle (*muʿjiza*), and the scholars are the heirs of the Prophets in sanctity and mercy. Nonetheless, they are differentiated by the extent of their endowment with Divine grace (*faḍl*), so understand this well.

Concerning God's saying, "*And a multitude from the later generations (are among the companions of the Right)*,"[339] our Shaykh (al-Tijānī), our means of access, the nourishment of our spirits, our supporter, the saintly pole (*quṭb*), the succor (*ghawth*), the Seal of Muḥammadan sainthood (*al-khatim al-Muḥammadī*), said: "They are our companions!" Consider this fairly, and you will find that Shaykh al-Tijānī acquired the complete inheritance (of the Prophet), so that the two multitudes came to be in the Muslim community. One multitude belongs to his grandfather, they being the companions of the God's Messenger, the peace and blessing of God on him. The other multitude belongs to him, may God be pleased with him, they being his own companions. My pen recoils from inscribing the rest of the implications here.

> In the secret of secrets are subtle details
> If we were to reveal them, our blood would be shed publicly.

Know that not even those with the lowest degree of faith can maintain the cessation of the Prophet's spiritual support (*madad*), or the waning of the light of his Prophecy. Our Shaykh (al-Tijānī) said, as recording in *al-Jāmiʿ* and *al-Jawāhir* (*al-Maʿānī*):

> Know that the Prophet, God's blessing and peace on him, used to impose general rules on the general populace (*al-ʿāma*) during his lifetime. Thus, when he declared something unlawful, it became unlawful for everybody. When he prescribed something, he prescribed it for everybody. This was the case for all the manifest rulings of the Sacred Law.

---

339 Qur'ān, 56:40.

In addition to all of these general rulings, he used to instruct the elite (*al-khāṣṣa*) with special knowledge, and he used to single out certain of his Companions and not others for certain affairs. This is something well-known and thoroughly recorded in the traditional reports concerning him.

When he was transferred to the abode of the Hereafter, the situation was therefore the same as it had been during his life in this world. He had begun to entrust to his community the special command for the elite, but without modification of the general command given to everybody. Modification of the general command ceased with his death, while the flood of his grace (*fayḍahu*) persisted in providing the special command to the elite.

Whoever imagines that all of his support for his community came to an end with his death, as in the case of other dead men, he is ignorant of the Prophet's rank. He is guilty of treating him indecently, and he is therefore in danger of dying as an unbeliever if he does not repent of his deluded conviction.

The Tijānī Sufi path and the way of gnosis

The goal of the Sufi path (*ṭarīqa*) of Sīdī Aḥmad al-Tijānī, may God be pleased with him, is, like other Sufi paths, the connection of the aspirant to God, Glorious and Exalted. Its goal is to take him by the hand for the duration of his journey until he enters the Divine Presence. That is the assiduous desire of every path. The *Ṭarīqa Aḥmadiyya Muḥammadiyya Tijāniyya* is distinguished from other paths by the plethora of blessing (*barakāt*), the power of its radiating lights, and the persistence of its luminosity. How could this not be so, when it is the path of the Seal of Saints? How excellent the glad tidings and spiritual provisions that have been enfolded in this path! And our information about this path comes from what the Messenger of God, the peace and blessing of God on him, himself informed our master Abū l-ʿAbbās (Aḥmad al-Tijānī), may God be pleased with him.

After this honor, there gushed forth the Tijānī gnosis, a flood from its wells on the hand of its possessor (Shaykh Ibrāhīm Niasse), may God be pleased with him. People then hastened to him and accepted him, and entered group upon group into this Sufi path at his hand. Even his previous enemies confessed that this was the possessor of the flood of gnosis (*ṣāḥib al-fayḍa*) that had been foretold. As the true owner of the flood, he gave spiritual training and elevation, and dispensed annihilation and persistence (in the Divine presence). He purified people and cleansed them, until all of them entered the presence of devotional worship and they came to stand before their Lord. That was his aspiration and work. He himself said: "As for my fellow travelers, my aim with them is to quench their thirst in the presence of God, the Generous Lord."

The Tijāniyya Sufi path is pure from all defects and innovation. (Shaykh Ibrāhīm) defended it from the prejudiced people, those misguided and misguiding others. He laid out a clear path for spiritual training, and who walks it arrives without trouble. The Shaykh said about this *Ṭarīqa*:

> The implementation of the litany (*wird*) of this *Ṭarīqa* by itself trains (the aspirant in gnosis). This is because he combines the plea for forgiveness (*istighfār*), prayer upon the Prophet (*ṣalāt ʿala-l-nabbī*), and the remembrance of God's Oneness (*haylala*, saying *lā ilāha ill-Allāh*). The meaning of the plea for forgiveness is removing oneself from sins and depravities. Prayer on the Prophet is to be endowed with excellent merits. The remembrance of God's Oneness is to witness the Divine manifestation, where God the Blessed and Exalted may manifest on the tongue of His servant with His words (in the Qurʾān), "*There is no god but God*," or "*There is no god but You*," or "*There is no god but I*."

If you look into these words, you will know that they cannot emerge except from a realized gnostic and most accomplished scholar, may God be pleased with him.

The *Kāshif al-ilbās* of Shaykh Ibrāhīm Niasse contains a detailed exposition, quite sufficient for our purposes, of spiritual training in our Sufi path. The Shaykh said:

> The sphere of spiritual training (*tarbiya*) revolves around two poles. The first is the establishment of the five ritual prayers in accordance

with their proper conditions. The second is the invocation of blessing on the Prophet throughout the night and at the beginning and end of the day, with the intention of obeying God's command to do so; and this with magnification, reverence and love (for the Prophet). This follows the strict observance of the obligatory daily litany (*wird*), which confirms the authenticity of being a Tijānī aspirant.

In the *Bughyat* (*al-Mustafīd*), one of the main books of the Tijānī path, the illustrious spiritual master and venerable guide, the father of endowments, al-Sayyid ʿArabi b. Sāʾiḥ, said on the subject of spiritual training:

"The sphere of spiritual training and purification in this noble Muḥammadan path of ours is centered on five practices. The first is the obligatory daily litany, without which entry into this path is invalid whatever a person's scholarly credentials. The second practice, linked to the first, is the attendance of the congregational remembrance; both the daily office (*waẓīfa*) and the weekly remembrance of "there is no god but God" (*haylala*) following the afternoon prayer on Friday.[340]

"The next essential practice is the attendance of the five daily ritual prayers. Certainly, all the practices mentioned here require careful observance of the stipulated conditions and proper modes of conduct in order to attain excellence and perfection. But of all the practices, the most imperative is the careful observance of the five daily prayers with their traditional elements as prescribed by the Sacred Law. You must comply with these stipulations as much as possible, perfectly fulfilling the basic elements of the prayer as established by customary practice.

"The next step in spiritual training is the aspirant's dedication to the invocation of blessing on the Prophet (*ṣalāt ʿala al-Nabī*) to the maximum extent possible, in all available moments. The best method thereof is with the Invocation of Opening what was Locked (*ṣalāt al-fātiḥ lima ughliq*), which is one of the most exalted and precious treasures.

---

340 Detailed descriptions of the obligatory Tijānī remembrances can be found in Appendix I of this book.

"Lastly, the aspirant undergoing spiritual training must persist in loving affection for the Prophet and gratitude to God Most High. He should rely only on Divine grace (*faḍl*), the sole means of realizing sainthood. In this way, sainthood is realized without the necessity of secluded retreat (*khalwa*), excessive strenuous exertion, or any of the other methods of training adopted after the earliest centuries of Islam.

"The type of spiritual path described here is what our master (Shaykh Aḥmad al-Tijānī) was commanded to follow by the master of existence, the fountain of spiritual assistance and generosity, God's peace and blessing upon him."

According to the *Jawāhir al-Maʿānī*, the Prophet informed our master and Shaykh (al-Tijānī) that he, God's blessing and peace on him, was the sole intermediary between him and God the Exalted. He also told him that he, God's blessing and peace on him, was definitely his spiritual sustainer, and the sole guardian in charge of his spiritual training in place of all the masters of the Sufi path. He informed him that not one of the spiritual masters had any favor to grant him, for everything he would receive from God would come by the assistance and mediation of the Prophet. Then he advised him, "Adhere to this path (*ṭarīqa*) without seclusion (*khalwa*) or separation from people, until you arrive to the spiritual station (*maqām*) promised you, while maintaining your (current) condition, without deprivation, constriction or a great deal of strenuous exertion."

The gnostic sage al-Buṣayrī, may God have mercy on him and be well pleased with him, indicated such a condition in verse:

> Excellence is not achieved by means
>   Of excessive abstinence nor asceticism
> If it is said, "That is the medicine," say
>   "The *kohl* of the healthy (for beautification) is not like the *kohl* used for eye-maladies."
> The one granted the right of disposition walks where he wills
>   Others walk like stones, shackled.

Sīdī al-ʿArabī b. Sā'iḥ said in *al-Jawāb al-Shāfī*:

"Whomever good fortune drives into entering this Aḥmadī Spiritual Path – whomever Divine Providence attracts to this chain of Muḥammadan transmission, whomever God's gracious favor has prepared to taste this great distinction, whomever His generosity has admitted to this marvelous chamber of treasure – his only remaining option is to bind himself to this greatest teacher (Shaykh al-Tijānī). He must finish himself at his door and cling to his threshold; and this by the path of love, submission and acceptance of His will and judgment. He must apply himself with diligence and perseverance to this noble Muḥammadan litany, observing its conditions and keeping within its precise limits. Then God the Exalted may grant him success.

"And this can be achieved while he remains in his normal condition, without secluded retreat, strenuous exertion or conventional spiritual exercises of other kinds. Success will either come upon him suddenly or take him by surprise. God the Exalted will favor him by removing the veil from his heart, and he will become united with the spirituality of the Shaykh, may God be pleased with him, or the spirituality of the Prophet, God's blessing and peace on him. Like this, his spiritual training comes by the flooding abundance (*istifāḍa*) from one of them, or from both of them together. '*That is the grace of God, which He gives to whom He wills; and God is the owner of infinite grace.*'"[341]

This is the meaning of what is found in the *Jawāhir al-Maʿānī* in regard to visualizing the presence of the Shaykh or the Prophet while performing the litanies for him who is able. The *Mīzāb al-Raḥma al-Rabbāniyya*, one of central books of the Tijāniyya, provides a lengthy explanation of this. The author said that God appoints for the aspirant a brother in the spiritual path, who will take on himself the burdens of his spiritual training. God the Exalted will show the aspirant the secret of his specialness and remove from between them the veil of the guide's human nature. He will travel with his guide toward God the Exalted, secretly and openly.

341 Qur'ān, 57:21.

Whoever attains spiritual illumination (*fataḥa*) in this manner, his light will be complete, for the illumination is commensurate with the one followed. This is why Shaykh Zarrūq said, "Each individual's illumination and light are commensurate with the illumination and light of the one he follows." If someone receives directly from the texts of the Qur'ān and the Sunnah, his illumination and light will be complete, provided that he is one of those qualified to receive from them. In doing so, however, he is failing to take advantage of the light and illumination of exemplary guidance. The Imams were wary of this approach, to the point where Ibn Madīnī,[342] may God have mercy on him, said, "Ibn Mahdī[343] used to go by the word of Mālik, while Mālik used to go by the word of Sulaymān b. Yasār,[344] and Sulaymān used to go by the word of 'Umar b. al-Khaṭṭāb. The doctrine of Mālik is therefore the doctrine of 'Umar, may God be pleased with him." Al-Junayd, may God have mercy on him, said:

> Whoever did not hear the traditions by sitting with scholars of understanding and by receiving proper manners from the morally refined, he will have a corrupting influence on those who follow him. God the Exalted said, "*Say, 'This is my way. On clear evidence, I call to God, I and all my followers. Glory be to God! And I am not among the idolaters.*"[345] And the Glorious One said: "*And this path of Mine is straight, so follow it. Follow not other ways, less you be parted from His way. This has He ordained for you, that you may fear Him.*"[346] Understand this well.

---

342 'Alī b. al-Madīnī (d. 848, Iraq) was a prominent Ḥadīth scholar who authored a work on the companions of the Prophet, *Kitāb al-Ma'rifat al-Ṣaḥāba*.

343 'Abd al-Raḥmān b. Mahdī was one of the students of the Imam Malik and his school of jurisprudence.

344 Sulayman b. Yasār (d. 733) was known as one of the seven scholars of Medina for his role in transmitting Islamic knowledge in the first century after the passing of the Prophet, peace be upon him. He was a slave of Maymuna bint al-Harith (the wife of the Prophet), who attained his freedom and became overseer of the Medina market during the time of 'Umar b. al-Khaṭṭāb.

345 Qur'ān, 12:108.

346 Qur'ān, 6:153.

There is no harm at this juncture in presenting some of our poems on this subject, for they contain useful advice for the truthful person. Some of the following poetic verses concern the spiritual traveler (*sālik*), while some concern the enraptured one (*majdhūb*).

Leave behind your dwellings and the beautiful women
    Leave the laden tables and soft couches
And keep company with any master successful in combining
    The Sacred Law (*sharī'a*) and the Divine Reality (*ḥaqīqa*)
A brother, pious and ascetic, uninterested
    In anything beyond what is right and proper
Beware of vain desires, and beware
    The brother wrapped up in the passing of time
(To the pious brother) grant him sovereign leadership, since you know
    There is none above him in this affair
Certainly, he has obliterated external appearance
    And has been made to arrive in the Presence of Holiness
Brought close, sanctified, and summoned
    By Divine permission, with the speech of everything near (to God)
When you see such a person, congratulations to you on the occasion of arrival
    For seeing him is a most glorious treasure to the eyes
The blessing of God, together with peace
    Upon the chosen one, from the first to the last

We also wrote:[347]

> Illumination comes in the presence of the distinguished folk (*al-aʿyān*)
> And your abandoning everything beside Him with utter conviction.

To us belong these verses as well:

> The arrived ones should not assume leadership
> Before permission is granted, for the secret is concealed
> I am pleased with the long silence
> For it is an indication of gnosis, and of an informed state
> There is no good in (mystical) interpretation at every gathering
> For secrets are removed with public mention
> May God, Lord of the Throne, care for us, by the secret of the Prophet's secret
> Upon him the blessing of God, for he is the disposer.

He who desires something more on this subject should keep company with the men of spiritual distinction and serve the people of spiritual perfection.

This is how Shaykh Ibrāhīm brought forth the explanation on the subject of spiritual training. May God be pleased with him and us on account of him.

347 These two verses are not in the published version of the *Kāshif* that this section otherwise reproduces but were handwritten in the margins of the text for this speech by Shaykh al-Tijānī Cissé. It is unclear whether these were verses composed by Shaykh Ibrāhīm or his grandson Shaykh al-Tijānī Cissé.

Breaths of Lights in the Statements of God's Exalted Folk

The light of the sun of the Divine Essence (*dhāt*) becomes manifest in the heart's mirror of the one seeking God, the one thirsting for the Real. This light outstrips the lights of the stars, the moon, and the sun: they are flung into the pitch-black abyss of nonexistence. This is because the seeker has erased all other existence and light, as in the words of the Most High, "*When the sun is folded up, and when the stars fall, losing their luster.*"[348] Indeed, this rising for judgment (*qiyāma*) for the seeker of God is a momentous event (*wāqiʿa*), not a stopping place. It is a semblance of the greater (Day of) Judgment (*al-qiyāma al-kubrā*). When the Hour's clear signs become evident, the imaginary and metaphorical lights of existence belonging to the creations are annihilated, melting away in the blazing light of God's infinite Essential Being (*dhāt-Allāh al-muṭlaqa*). With the manifestation of the Absolute Exalted Truth, the (Day of) Rising is established. All existence other than His Holy Existence passes away. And what is postponed for others becomes the immediate reality for the seeker of God.

Ibn ʿAjība said in the Īqāẓ: "The sign of the perfection of the gnostic is his comportment (ādāb) in seeking, in expansion and contraction, and in denial and provision. Among everything that the Real, glorious is He, gives to His servants, He gives nothing better than the acceptance of their righteous deeds."

When the sun appears in the daytime, you do not see the stars. Similarly, when the sun of gnosis shines forth, extinguished are the traces (āthār) and vestiges (*rusūm*) (of creation). Nothing remains except the Ever-Living, Self-Subsisting. It has been said:

When the morning becomes plain, its light registers
With fading light of the stars.

---

348 Qur'ān, 81:1-2.

It has also been said:

Between myself and the Real, there remains no explanation
    No evidence, no signs of proof
This manifestation of the suns of the Real is a conquering fire
    I came to glow in the brilliant luminosity of the Sovereign Lord
No one knows the Real except who knows by Him
    No one knows the antiquity of the conversion in annihilation
One is not informed of the Originator (simply) by His workmanship
    You saw what happened with the Prophet in his time
This is an expression from those of singularity
    Endowed with gnosis secretly and openly.

Shaykh Aḥmad al-Tijānī on Divine Witnessing

The Hidden Pole (*al-quṭb al-maktūm*) explained the meaning of the report (of God's words to the Prophet), "My servant does not cease approaching me with supererogatory worship until I love him, and when I love him, I become his hearing by which he hears" till the end of the *ḥadīth*. The following citation is from the *Jawāhir al-maʿānī*.

> The meaning of "until I love him" is as follows. God's love for a servant entails the flood of love upon him from God's holy Essential Being. This is the most exalted of favors, and this is where the journey for all travelers ends. Whoever arrives here has all of his worldly and otherworldly needs completed. When He said, "when I love him," He is saying, "I overwhelm him in love of My Essential Being," to the extent of God's words, "*He loves them, and they love Him.*"[349] Were it not for His love, glorious and exalted is He, for them, they would not have arrived at the love of His Essential Being.
>
> As for His words, "and when I love him, I become his hearing," till the end of the narration, the meaning is as follows. The servant sees

349 Qur'ān, 5:54.

in himself a divine power as if he were the divine, sacred, Essential Being, with all of its Attributes and Names; as if he were He, but he is not He. However, God the Glorious and Exalted has poured on him of the light of His Attributes and Names in order to raise his station. Thus does he come to carry what the entirety of the creation cannot carry because of its weight. This is why some of the gnostics have said, "The one for whom is unveiled a grains worth of divine unity (*tawḥīd*) carries the heavens and the two earths in his eyelashes," because he has been raised to this station by divine power. He sees by God, as if his bodily presence was the Essential Being of God the Exalted. He hears by God.

The indication of seeing and hearing by God is that in one glance, he sees all of existence, from the Divine throne to earthly canopy, with not a single grain hidden from him. He fulfills what is due to each existence, from behind and in front, to the right and left, above and below. He sees all of this in one instant, and he sees existence as a unique jewel of extraordinary apportioning, and (he sees) free of mirrors that would change its states, composition, movement, or color. All of this he sees in one glance, in one instant, in every direction, without mistaking a single grain. The reason for this vision is that eye of the spirit (*rūḥ*) has been opened. If the eye of the spirit should be opened in his bodily presence, all the creations and worlds appear before him, and not one vision is confounded. This is the meaning of seeing by God the Exalted.

Hearing by God the Exalted is when a person hears all the enunciations of existence in all of the worlds, with all of their different glorifications and remembrances (of God) in one instant, without obfuscation despite the plethora of enunciations and glorifications. It is as if, for each enunciation, he hears nothing other than it. Audition normally cannot distinguish one voice if there should be many voices all at once. But the comportment (*salk*) demanded of this state is to hear all of the articulations and glorifications of the existent beings without confusion.

Shaykh al-Islam Ibrāhīm Niasse on Divine Manifestation in Created Forms (*tajallī ṣūrī*)[350]

Divine manifestation in created forms is of three degrees. The lowest of them is what is presented to the aspirant honored with arrival in the Divine Presence (*wuṣūl*). He witnesses the figurative existence as the eye of the actual existence. He sees the Divine manifestation in the mirror (of creation), but he sees neither the mirror nor Him who manifests therein. The intermediary degree is what the gnostics witness when coming to sobriety and persistence (*baqā'*). They see the Real in an impossible form. Ibn Fāriḍ said:

> Beware of denying all form
> Among frailties and impossible conditions

The highest degree is what the Messenger of God, peace and blessing of God on him, witnessed during the Night Journey (and Ascension) when he saw God in the form of a beardless youth (*shāb amrad*).[351]

But the Divine Essential Being (*dhāt*) is infinite existence (*al-wujūd al-muṭlaq*) that elevates the aspirant above the Divine manifestation in forms. The aspirant arrives to essential interiorities where there is nothing seen and nothing manifest. Thus does he truly arrive to God, "*The Real has come, and falsehood has perished, for falsehood is bound to perish.*"[352]

The essence of the Essence (*dhāt al-dhāt*) is the presence of the greatest veil, or the flood (*al-fayḍ*), the greatest spirit (*al-rūḥ al-akbar*). To this presence belongs the secret of the Divine Essential

---

350 The following passage was a letter written in response to a disciple's question on the subject, and is found in Shaykh Ibrāhīm Niasse, *Jawāhir al-rasā'il*, I, 115-117.

351 This was the narration of the Prophet's Companion Ibn ʿAbbās concerning the Prophet's ascension. For further discussion, see W. Williams, "*Tajallī wa-Ru'ya:* A Study of Anthropomorphic Theophany and *Visio Dei* in the Hebrew Bible, the Qur'ān and Early Sunnī Islam" (PhD dissertation, Near Eastern Studies, University of Michigan, 2008), 121. Muslim scholars often were careful to contextualize this vision (*ru'ya*) within larger understandings of God's incomparability to His creation. See https://islamqa.info/ar/answers/152835/براءة-اهل-السنة-من-تشبيه-الله-بشاب-امرد. Accessed 6 July 2022.

352 Qur'ān, 17:81.

Being, a second existence, the existence of existence, the support of existence, the light of existence, the Muḥammadan reality (*al-ḥaqīqa al-Muḥammadiyya*).

The presence of Divine Uniqueness (*al-Aḥadiyya*) is the manifestation of the Divine Essential Being to Itself by Itself. There is no description of this except *"He is God the Unique."*[353] The presence of singularity (*al-wāḥidiyya*) is the manifestation of the Divine Essential Being to the Muḥammadan reality. Knowing the secret of appearance and hiddenness is when the servant knows that appearance is hiddenness, and hiddenness is appearance. This is because you know that appearance is manifestation, so understand well.

Pre-eternity is an expression of what has not ceased to be, and post-eternity is an expression of what will never be changed. In reality, both are the same, and refer to the persistence of the secret of the cosmological presences (*sirr al-ḥaḍarāt*). As for the world of the unseen, this is part of witnessing, and perhaps both could be explained by my previous explanation of the world of the creation and that of the command. The creation (*al-kawn*) is the place of Divine manifestation, that which is pervaded by Him, the figurative being made real by the Real Being, and such is the servant. Before his creation, the servant was not other than God, and with his creation he remains in the state in which he was. This is why it has been said:

The Lord is truth, and the servant is truth
    I wish I knew one so entrusted (*mukallif*)
If you say, "servant," the servant is dead
    If you say say, "Lord," I am the one entrusted.

But the truth is obviously that the Lord is not like the servant, and the servant is unable to be the Lord. What is correct is that to be a servant is to be among the creation. Divine longing (*shawq*) is a state of love and ecstasy, an overwhelming obliteration of the self that strikes the heart of the servant from presence of Divine compulsion. The servant

353 Qur'ān, 112:1.

removes himself from all personal choice, sometimes in honored proximity with the Real, sometimes in honored proximity with our Master the Messenger of God, the peace and blessing of God on him, and sometimes in the Shaykh (al-Tijānī).

The primordial (Divine) identity (*al-māhiyya al-hayūlī*) is the Pure Essential Being *(al-dhāt al-sādhij)*, a sea of blindness and effacement where there is no identity. As for the (assertive) Divine Identity (*huwiyya*), it is the presence of "He" (*huwa*).[354] The Name "He" among the gnostics is among the Names of the God's Essential Being. Its presence is understood by the words of God, "*That is because He is the Real.*"[355]

Intoxication (*sukr*)[356] is the enraptured one's experience of liberation in the state of his absence from the creation and presence with the Real. Love (*al-maḥabba*) is the attachment of the heart to the Exalted Essential Being of God, enamored with Him for His sake, not for any other purpose. This is not the case except for the perfected gnostics. May God make us among them by His blessing.

Conclusion

Let us conclude this discourse of Divine longing, a discourse that does not desire an ending, with mention of the words of the Seal of Saints, Shaykh Aḥmad al-Tijānī, may God be pleased with him. You will not find the following words in any book.

> I was pushed forward by a burst (*duf'a*) from the divine presence. My beginning became my end, my end my beginning. My entirety became my every particle, and my every particle became my entirety. I became

---

354 Shaykh Ibrāhīm is here subtly contrasting two words meaning "identity": *māhiyya* and *huwiyya*; literally "whatness" and "He-ness." The understanding seems to be that the "what" of God cannot be delimited, but that the Being of God can be described as the singular true reality, the Real. For more on contrasting concepts of divine identity, see Sachiko Murata, *The Tao of Islam* (Albany: SUNY Press, 1992), 66.

355 Qur'ān, 31:30.

356 The printed version of the *Jawāhir al-rasā'il* has the word *sirr* ("secret") instead of *sukr*, apparently a mistake corrected in Shaykh al-Tijānī Cissé's written speech here.

> Him, and He me, but as becoming of Him, and not as becoming of me. At that moment, if I were asked a million separate questions, I would have given only one answer. Then I became like the niche of light (*miṣbāḥ*).

Shaykh al-Islām Ibrāhīm Niasse was attached to this statement, saying, "These words are the reason for my being pleased to have him as our Shaykh."

There is no doubt that such words would not emerge except from a most distinguished guidepost, the eye of sainthood (ʿayn al-walāya), may God be pleased with him. It is no small wonder, for the witness (to al-Tijānī's words) was the most famous scholar, the most luminous saintly pole, the most glittering star, the unique of his era, the singular of his age, the profound erudite, our master the Shaykh of Islam, al-Ḥājj Ibrāhīm b. al-Ḥājj ʿAbdallāh al-Tijānī, may God be pleased with him. And I should like to mention here a spiritual witnessing (*mashhad*) among many belonging to this pole of saintly aspirations. And with this, I will end this speech, so that our conclusion will be like fragrant musk. He said, may God be pleased with him:

> A momentous occurrence happened to the humble servant writing this in the year 1350 (1931/1932) after the Hijra of Muḥammad, upon him blessing and peace. It was that I came to abide (*makathtu*) for a hundred thousand years among the days of the Lord. There I heard the purest, pre-eternal speech in intimate conversation. I became bewildered and restless, as both rapture and longing were joined in me.
>
> Then I plunged headlong into the Divine Presence, and I witnessed there the reality of the reality of the reality of the Reality, in utter essentiality, exclusivity, and blind effacement. Nothing was left of sensory feelings. I dwelled like this for two hundred thousand years. Then something was with me. The existence became particularized from me like shadows or smoke. And I sought after this existence, and then I was with the Messenger, from the Divine Essential Being (*dhāt*), the servant of the Divine Essential Being and Its secret. And He came close to me and stayed suspended until I disappeared in

him. He became my essence. Then I was overcome with joy, for I was the beloved of the Divine Essential Being, Its secret, Its servant, Its longing. I was that which held Its comprehensive station (*martabatahā al-jāmiʿa*), to whom the perfection of the Divine Essential Being was manifest. I resided in my state of rapture for one million years. In this manifestation in the unseen (*ghayb*), I did not find any servant of the Divine Essential Being except myself. But then there was another manifestation, unseen out of the unseen, and I saw a majestic awe (*jalāl*) in the ultimate beauty (*jamāl*). In this presence of the unseen of the unseen, I was called forth and named, "O Aḥmad al-Tijānī!" I knew for certain that there was no desire of the Real after the secret than for me (within al-Tijānī's reality). I kept company with this servant of the Divine Essential Being, and I helped him and aided him for two million years.

Then God made me the father of humanity (*abū l-bashar*), and the spiritual support (*madad*) for the entirety of existent beings, the Adam of souls and spirits. I carried the trust (*amāna*), and I was called to, "*O Dāwūd, surely We have made you the khalīfa on the earth.*"[357] I looked at the earth, and saw its state, the worlds of sense and of meaning, and then the celestial gathering, and the lower gathering. "*We built the heaven with might, and We it is who made the vast expanse. And We have laid out the earth. Gracious is He who spread it out! And all things We have created in pairs, that haply you may reflect. Therefore, flee to God. I am a warner to you from Him. Set up no other gods besides God. I am a warner to you from Him.*"[358] Then I came back to my sensory feeling, and it was if the time period of the occurrence was between the even and the odd. Glory to God the Majestic. He selects whom He wills for what He wills, and no one outstrips His wisdom. "*And He is not asked about what He does, but they are the ones asked.*"[359]

---

357 Qur'ān, 38:26.

358 Qur'ān, 51:47-51.

359 Qur'ān, 21:23.

With this I conclude. I ask God the Blessed and Exalted to make us among those who know Him and understand Him, to make us among the elite of the elite, those passed away in Him if He should cause them to pass away, those persisting in Him if He should cause them to remain. May He guard us from being absent from Him, and not allow ourselves to be fatigued in being present with Him. We ask Him by the presences of prophecy, sainthood, and their *khalīfa*, that He provide us with gnosis, by His spacious, lordly capacity, that He take us by the hands and attach our hearts to Him, Blessed and Exalted is He.

> O God, bless our master Muḥammad, the opener of what was closed, the seal of what was past, the helper of truth by the truth, the guide to Your straight path, and on his family, commensurate with his worth and grandeur.

www.ingramcontent.com/pod-product-compliance
Lightning Source LLC
Chambersburg PA
CBHW060355080526
44583CB00012B/325
* 9 7 8 1 7 3 3 9 6 3 1 7 6 *